Just Thought you SHOULD KNOW

Guidance for Independent Artists from an Independent Artist on How to 'Make It' in the Music Industry

Matt Annecharico

*Matilday,
Thank you for letting
me be a small part
of your journey.*

DREAMSCOPE INSIGHTS

LONDON | LOS ANGELES

First published in Great Britain in 2019 by Dreamscope Insights - London

First published in the United States in 2019 by Dreamscope Insights - Los Angeles

Dreamscope Insights is a trading-as company of
Dreamscope Media Group Limited
71-75 Shelton Street, London WC2H 9JQ

First edition

Edited By Greg Brown

Illustration by Matt Annecharico
Cover design by Matin Fellani

Library of Congress Cataloging-in-Publication Data:

Annecharico, Matt | Brown, Greg, editor
        Just Thought You Should Know; Guidance for Independent Artists from an Independent Artists on how to 'Make It' in the Music Industry / by Matt Annecharico; edited by Greg Brown
LCCN 2019909623   ISBN 978-1-9161684-0-4 (pbk.) - ISBN 978-1-9161684-1-1 (ebk.)
LC record available at https://lccn.loc.gov/2019909623

A catalogue record for this book is available from the British Library.

I want to thank all of the hard-working people who I've had on my artist team over the years: the musicians, managers, producers, engineers, agents, legal teams, media outlets, collaborators, and so many more. A special shout out to the people who work with me at Dreamscope. I want to thank my family and friends for their unconditional support; I couldn't have done anything in life without it. Finally, I want to thank all of the people throughout the world who allow me into their lives through my music. You inspire me in so many ways, even when you don't know it.

Love,

This book is dedicated to all the artists, musicians, and bands out there who have ever had the dream of being on stage and earning an income from their art. Dreams really can come true when you buckle down, work hard, and never lose your vision and tenacity.

CONTENTS

I. Before We Get Started, I've Gotta Be Honest 1

II. Define Your Own Narrative ("WHY") 14

Start with Why 14
Case Study: Disney's Magic Kingdom 15
Case Study: "Mirrors" 17
Case Study: Band A 19
Develop Your Artist Brand 20
The Power of Motivations 22
Four Major Indicators of Motivation 24
Study, Study, Study 25
Stay Focused 27
Dreamscope's Artist Checklist 29

III. Assemble the Troops ("HOW") 32

YOU are a Business. Get Over It! 32
Smoke and Mirrors 35
No, You Can't Do It Alone 37
Working With Your Team 39
Let's Talk Record Labels 43
Let's Talk Digital Distribution 49
Let's Talk Marketing Tools 52
What Is Your Market 72
Let's Talk Music Publishing 74
Let's Talk Music Tech 77

IV. Start Earning ("WHAT") 84

Your Results 84
Music Rights and Copyrights Explained 85
Composition Royalty Flow Chart 90

Direct to Fan Marketing 91

Everyone's A Damn Critic 93

Don't Forget WHY...95

Rejuvenate, Revitalise, Get Inspiration, and Repeat.........96

V. To Sum It Up   98

Letter to a New Artist 100

Additional Resources   104

Further Reading..104

Blank Contracts 105

Appendix 1:   106

Sample Record Contract clauses   106

Appendix 2:   117

Commentary on Record Contract clauses   117

Glossary   123

Before We Get Started

Alright, full disclosure: I have never achieved worldwide fame. I haven't come anywhere near making a million dollars over the course of my life. I've never had stadium tours. I've never even been so much as nominated for a Grammy (although I'm a voting member - that's gotta count for something). While I've achieved my own definition of success, I still only hear "you look like a famous singer" regularly which basically means I don't even make the 'D List'. So why should you take advice from me about your music career? Well, the truth is maybe you shouldn't. Maybe you should be reading some of the books written by or even about one of the musical greats telling you about their epic rise to stardom. Or maybe you should be watching one of the thousands of documentaries that show some music superstar sitting in their dimly-lit, multi-million dollar recording studio reminiscing about their career highlights. Might be quicker and more interesting for you. After all, that's what you want, isn't it?

Or maybe what you should be asking yourself is why you are reading these books or watching these documentaries in the first place. Is it just for enjoyment? Is it for inspiration? Is it to find that secret formula to becoming a world-renowned pop star so that you can make millions of dollars, buy fancy cars, and big houses? T– The reason you might consider taking some advice from me is because I am you. Right now, at this very moment, I'm fighting to make money doing what I love - music. In maybe I am a bit more experienced than you and in some cases maybe I'm

1

I've Gotta Be Honest

not. But I've learned a lot over the years and I've had a lot of experiences that I hope can prove useful for you as you navigate your career. People always give me crap for having a story for everything. Well, to understand why you may want to consider reading a book by me about how to be a successful artist, I've gotta tell you a story. As I always say (and usually fail miserably at), I'll keep it brief...

To say that I came from humble beginnings would be an understatement. I grew up on the south side of Phoenix, Arizona in a predominantly Mexican-American neighbourhood with my two very young parents and my sister who is one year younger than me. It was normal to go to bed at night while hearing the sounds of close-by gun shots. We were surrounded (literally) by murderers, drug cartels, thieves and the like. It was a dog-eat-dog environment. Without getting into too much personal information, suffice it to say that I also grew up around constant domestic abuse to top it all off. My mom, the bread winner in the family, worked at the telephone company. She would leave for work before we woke up in the mornings and she didn't get home until just before we had to go to bed, if we were lucky. For most of my childhood my dad was a pool salesmen but following a mysterious layoff that I don't care to ever ask about, he found it hard to find and/or hold onto a job and I suspect he leaned on his other nefarious "side jobs" that he'd always done for extra money. Still, we didn't have a lot. One winter my primary school teacher came to school with warm clothes because, despite the cold, I had been coming to school every day with shorts and a t-shirt. It was a tough childhood but it was all I knew so things that would shock a person now were considered normal for me. But it wasn't all bad.

On the weekend, my parents would drive my sister and I to the Paradise Valley area of North Phoenix, which was culturally the polar opposite to where we lived, where we would stay with my mother's parents who had a very comfortable upper middle-class lifestyle. My Grandma, a retired manager from the telephone company and the daughter of a cobbler,

Mom posing me for an artist who was painting my portrait.

insisted that I had good shoes at all times and my Grandpa always made sure that there was plenty of Oreo cookies and ice cream in the house. My sister and I had our own rooms at their house, which was a nice reprieve from the small room we shared together at home. We'd go out to dinners with them often. Nothing fancy but still something I was not used to doing and when we did eat dinners at their house my Grandma made beautiful, home-cooked meals we enjoyed while sitting around the dinner table. Again, something that I was not used to. Our Saturday nights were then capped off by watching the CBS television shows "Dr. Quinn Medicine Woman" and "Touched by an Angel" before finally going to bed so that we could get up in the morning to go to church.

At church, a small Protestant denomination called Christ The King Lutheran, I learned that even Jesus came from humble beginnings and was still able to do great things with his life. I remember many things from my days growing up in a church but one memory that stands out more than anything was the sense of community, acceptance and love. Although the amazing baked goods made by the sweet grandmas of the congregation were always a highlight, too! As kids at church we were free to run and play and just be ourselves the way kids should be allowed to be. I loved going to church. Over the years my pastors quickly saw my interest in the arts and gave me constant opportunities to explore them. I wrote articles in the church newsletter that went out through the U.S. Postal Service every

Just Thought You Should Know

month (before e-mail was widely used. Weird, right?). I was in every children's play they put on. Like so many other artists, I was maybe six years old when my church gave me my first opportunity to sing in public. During rehearsals the Music Director gave me a part in singing "Silent Night" and all the kids laughed at me as I muddled through it. A child prodigy I was not. As a teenager the congregation elected me to church Council President, the youngest ever in Lutheran Church history, where I served for two years. I even started my own Contemporary worship service ("contemporary" being the word of the day during that time frame when the church was fighting to attract a younger audience). To say that I got my start in the church would be a significant understatement.

While all of this was happening, though, I had other ambitions. I wanted to be an actor. I didn't understand the full breadth of what it meant to be an actor but I didn't care. Actors were loved. They got to pretend and make-believe and I wanted to do that, too. How did they make those angels glow at the end of "Touched by an Angel"? It was magical and I wanted to be part of it. My Great Uncle Art Annecharico had his own production company in Hollywood, The Arthur Co. Over the years he has won three Academy Awards and produced such shows as "Airwolf", "The Munsters Today", "Dragnet", and many others. He is a bit of an idol of mine. At times a seemingly mythical being whom I only ever spoke to on the phone and saw at weddings. Speaking to me about becoming an actor, he once said to me "go learn first". I hated to hear that. It annoyed me. I wanted him to teach me and give me my big break. My eight or nine year old mind just couldn't understand what he was actually saying.

Headshot circa 1995

Still I carried on.

Over the years and from an incredibly early age I did quite a lot of stage acting in theatres of all sizes, in school, and in church. I booked radio commercial jobs for companies like United Way, television shows such as History Channel's "Wild West Tech", and several independent films thanks to my very talented agent. But very early in my acting career I ran into my first scam from a company claiming to help make people stars in the film

Filming The History Channel's "Wild West Tech"

and television business. I had a fancy photo shoot and begged my mom to pay them money to "represent" me, which she did. But, of course, my eight or nine year old mind didn't listen to my Great Uncle Art so I didn't understand why I wasn't being booked for jobs.

When I was nine years old my dad took me to a competition that had people of all ages and disciplines performing for some pretty big name casting and talent agencies (like, legitimate ones). I had to prepare a monologue and I cannot recall which one I had prepared to do but an hour before my spot I decided to change it and ended up doing a monologue from the film Titanic, which had only just been released. Before going out, some man walked up to me backstage where I was alone and shocked the hell out of me.

MAN: You look pretty nervous, kid. You alright?

ME: Yeah I'm fine.

MAN: Here, maybe this will help.

That was the first time I was ever offered cocaine. I don't think I even replied and instead opted to turn around and walk away in horror. Anyway, I walked out and did the monologue and a casting agent by the name of Faith Hibbs-Clark, who went on to do the casting for such projects as 2017's Transformers film, gave me her card and asked me to call her. I didn't realise at the time but she was really one of the first to shape what would become my career in the entertainment business. She offered me private in-home acting lessons and taught me how to be diligent, intentional without seeming so, and how to comb through every line of a script to find the changes in emotion. There were so many lessons that would ultimately cross over into my music career. But of course these lessons were not free and unfortunately were not financially sustainable for my family. Despite this, Faith and I stayed in touched for many years. She is a wonderful woman.

Still I carried on.

Just Thought You Should Know

I continued with my acting career and got to play such roles as Nick Bottom from *Midsummer Night's Dream*, which I got to play on one of the only two replicas of Shakespeare's Globe Theatre located on the campus of Southern Utah University in Cedar City, Utah. I played Romeo in *Romeo and Juliet*, Danny Zuko in *Grease!*, Joseph in *Joseph and the Amazing Technicolor Dreamcoat*, Oz in *The Wizard of Oz*. I was having a ball playing load of roles in productions with big budgets and in productions with small ones. A true thespian. In between gigs, I had met a man named Bryce Budge, a professional piano player who was hired to play music at my church. He found out that I performed and invited me over to his lower-middle class home where he had a home studio, something that was still a new concept for the non-rich and famous. I couldn't resist the opportunity. When I first saw it, I was mesmerised by it. The space was beautiful. He had set up two different keyboards, a recording console, and quite a lot of outboard gear. It was magical. He regularly recorded not only other artists trying to break into the industry but he also recorded is own instrumental albums which he sold at his gigs. He was regularly booked to play gigs all over Arizona, and I was in awe of his talent, the fact that he was making money from his music and the fact that he was paying attention to me. He asked me if I wanted to travel with him on his gigs as a roadie and I jumped at the chance, quickly learning how to take care of musical equipment, how to set up and tear down live sound equipment, and quite a lot about running live sound. Best of all was that I got to hear him play. It was so beautiful. It was the first time I'd ever witnessed someone perform music from the heart, every single time, despite the fact that he wasn't making much money from it. He did it because he wasn't born to do anything else. That was that. The money was almost secondary.

In my early teens, I was offered the chance to record an album with a small team of passionate musicians at Campfire Christian Ministries. The opportunity came out of left field. I had been working as an actor and I had never received any training on being a singer. But I went with it and took them up on the opportunity. I only got to write one song for the album and we did a pretty big church tour to promote the album. It became a local success. One day when I was in Minnesota rehearsing for a Central American tour I got a call from a friend of mine who told me he'd heard the song I wrote for the project played on the national Christian radio station K-Love. I was ecstatic. Around this time Bryce told me "Matt-o! You've got the bug!". He was right. I loved singing and people seemed to really react positively to it. I wanted to explore it more so I continued writing songs. At that point in my life I was annoyed that I was becoming the poster boy for how to be a good Christian boy even though I felt the complete opposite. I never broke the law or did anything bad but Matt, that good Christian boy, was seemingly perfect, something I didn't feel like Matthew was. Thus came the idea for my next project "Mirrors".

I wanted to start to build my own in-home recording studio like the one Bryce had but I didn't know what kind of equipment I needed in order

Performing during a festival tour

to do so. So I called up local record labels and asked to tour their studios. The first one, MakeShift Records in Scottsdale, Arizona, warmly welcomed me into their facilities and showed me around. It was amazing. Just like what you'd imagine - dimly lit rooms, loads of fancy outboard gear and computers, several recording rooms with several rooms used for offices. I felt like I didn't belong. Afterwards they asked me if I sang, to which I replied that I did. They asked to hear my

stuff, so I ran out to my car to grab my press kit, which I carried around with me, and gave it to them before heading on my way. Several weeks later, to my amazement, they offered me a record contract for one project. I considered it for weeks and finally accepted after we had discussions about what this project would be. I had a very clear vision and I didn't want to just record a pop album for the sake of it. I wanted there to be more depth to it and so I got the label to agree to donate to $1 from every sale of the album to the Muscular Dystrophy Association in my cousin's honour. My cousin had passed away from the disease six years prior and I promised him I'm carry on his legacy. My life was changed.

Just Thought You Should Know

What transpired was a whirlwind. I was nominated for several music awards at the LA Music Awards as well as the Hollywood Music In Media Awards and the Charlotte Music Awards, I was doing red carpet interviews in Hollywood in the shadow of the famous Capital Records building, I was offered interviews and performance opportunities all over the world, and I was being paid to perform. Not a tremendous

amount, but being booked to do a 40-minute set on a massive stage that many artists only dream about for a fee of $2,500.00 seemed pretty good to me. I was blessed, and I knew it. I didn't intend on this happening. I certainly didn't think it was possible. Yet here I was.

Cover art for "Mirrors" album

One night, we had a gig at a venue called Life on Wilshire in Los Angeles. This particular tour was already special to me because Bryce, the man who had mentored me for so many years, got to come with me as my Music Director and keyboardist. Just before we got to Los Angeles, the music industry went into full-on shock mode at the death of Michael Jackson. I'd

been to Hollywood hundreds of times at this point but this was nothing like I'd ever seen before. Every car had its windows rolled down blaring his music, billboards, signs and the side of buildings had memorials for the King of Pop. The night before the gig, we went to where it star was on the Walk of Fame just outside of Grauman's Chinese Theatre in Hollywood (now called TCL Chinese Theatre) and, to our amazement, at 3 a.m., there was a massive line that stretched around the block of mourners waiting to leave flowers and take

Performing with Bryce at Life On Wilshire in Los Angeles, California

pictures next to his star. It was unbelievable. My manager told me that we had to add a Michael Jackson song to our set, which I did reluctantly. The song was "You Are Not Alone". Of course I knew of the song, but I didn't know it well enough to perform it, and I certainly didn't feel confident performing it in this environment. Just in case,

I wrote the first line of verse one on my left palm, and the first line of verse two on my right hand. I was so nervous. We nailed it, though, with a standing ovation. The sound engineer that night was an engineer on several Celine Dion projects. He told me afterwards that I needed to record that song. I thanked him, but in my mind, I was saying "no way". Michael's music was perfect and, in my opinion, should be left alone. A year later, my new manager had spoken to the Jackson family, who was putting on an event in Gary, Indiana where Michael had grown up, to commemorate the date of Michael's passing. Keith Jackson, Michael's first cousin, had heard about what we did in LA and they asked me to come perform at the

With Michael Jackson's cousin, Keith

memorial. When my manager called me I was on a date in Las Vegas. I had to bail on the poor guy but he was very understanding several days later after I had told him what happened. I was again, asked to record the song but this time by Michael's family. I couldn't say no this time and so I recorded it and donated the money I earned to The Trevor Project, a 24 hour crisis hotline for LGBT youth. What an experience that was!

In 2013, when nearly done with my third album, my partner had the opportunity to move to London to get a master's degree and asked me to come with. I decided that it might be a great idea to finally obtain a degree before the whirlwind of releasing an album kicked off again, soI moved to London. Within six months I was asked to write, produce, and record a song commemorating Her Majesty Queen Elizabeth II as the longest reigning monarch in British history along with West End actress Patty Boulaye. As part of the process, I had three etiquette lessons over high tea with the Queen's niece, Her Royal Highness Princess Katarina, which was quite the experience. The project was turning into a big affair however, due to budget constraints, it was called off before we ever hit the studio.

While in London obtaining my undergraduate degree in Popular Music, I was encouraged to start my own record label, something I had never

Just Thought You Should Know

considered. I decided that if I were to do this, I didn't want to just start a label and be like everyone else. I wanted to break the mould. In 2016, my business partner and I founded Dreamscope Media Group Limited, which we refer to as the first truly modern record label. We believe that a record label should focus more on being a services company for artists rather than putting so much energy into making products for the general public.

So there you have it. That's my story. Well, most of it. You can read more on my artist website, www.officialmatt.com. For personal reasons, I left out the stories about managers stealing money and contacts from me, lawsuits I've had to file, and the like. Getting screwed over by people supposedly looking out for my best interest was very much a part of my journey, but it's not something I enjoy reminiscing about. I don't totally blame the people who did these things. I didn't listen to my Uncle Art and lacked the knowledge I needed to protect myself and - let's face it - when people see an opportunity to jump on the gravy train they typically do. The bottom line is that no artist should have to go through those kinds of things anymore. My goal is to make sure that artists don't get screwed over like I did. And that is why I've written this book. In all my years of reading I've never found a book that really looked at being an artist in today's music industry from a more holistic stand point. There are many fantastic music law books as well as many music business books and the like but never one that actually taught me how to be successful in a way that felt attainable and real to me. Is this book complete? No, I would not say that it is. Some of the pointers and tips may not work for everyone and I understand. The goal is to get you thinking. The goal is to open the door for you but it's up to you to walk through it. Don't try to learn absolutely everything about the industry but do strive to have a basic understanding of the fundamentals and then play to your strengths.

Record labels used to be the gatekeepers to market for artists but that hasn't been the case in many years thanks to technology and so to continue acting this way, as most do, to me was futile. Then, of course, there was the drama of file sharing which killed the recorded music industry and was largely responsible for the creation of the infamous 360 Degree Record

Deal, which, in my opinion, is disgusting. The idea of these deals is "without us, you would not be where you are today so anything you do in the entertainment industry, we should get a cut of". I have been offered many of these deals from indie labels as well as major labels but I've always turned them down. The notion that a record label should get a large percentage of my income from activities that didn't even involve my music seemed absurd. Not to mention giving up so many of my own rights to my career including the copyright to my own name, in one case. No way! Moreover, an artist just starting out in their career who is offered a 360 Deal may (if they are lucky) only see 12 percent royalties. It's madness and I wanted no part. To the contrary, artists today need record labels for their connections to industry, for their knowledge, for development, and for guidance along with some of the more typical functions of a record label such as marketing. They don't need labels to record, mix, and release music. So Dreamscope offers Artists Development and Production deals as sort of an on-the-job-training where artists experience the process during a short-term contract. It's bold. It's modern. And it's working.

Just like my thought process when I established Dreamscope, in writing this book I want to redefine what books on the modern music industry are like for artists. I'll avoid using convoluted terms when possible and speak to you artist to artist which will hopefully make the concepts I cover in this book more real and attainable. Maybe through some of my experiences in finding myself as a creative person in the business world, you'll be able to find yourself too. I hope that this book both educates and inspires you. I hope that it makes you think about things in ways that you otherwise wouldn't have. I hope that it provides you with a practical and, as I said, a more holistic approach to being an artist in today's music industry. Most importantly, I want this book to give you hope that you can make money from your music career. It's hard work, but guess what - you can do it! What follows are many of my own personal secrets based on my experiences that I'm sharing simply because I just thought you should know.

11

The Golden Circle

WHY

HOW

WHAT

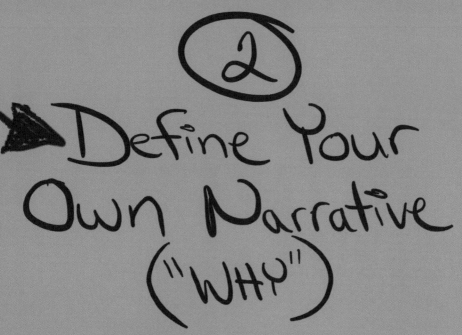

Define Your Own Narrative ("WHY")

Start with Why

Things are about to get really theoretical and deep for a moment, but go with me on this ride. Throughout this book, I'm going to regularly borrow on the concepts of a very inspiring man many people in the business world have looked to for advice. His name is Simon Sinek, and I'll apply his principles to your business as an artist. Sinek wrote a book called *Start with Why* that completely changed my life. It made me question everything about what I was doing with my career. In questioning everything, I actually found clarity. In fact, the book shaped the very fundamentals of my record label, Dreamscope Media Group, but also helped me to better understand myself as an artist so I just thought you should know about it, too.

Sinek's theory is called The Golden Circle. The general idea is that when someone talks about themselves - let's say as a solo artist - they typically say WHAT they do and usually HOW they do it, but they never truly get to WHY they do it, which might be the most important aspect. Here's the kicker: studies show successful people do this process backwards.

Successful people talk about WHY they do what they do, then HOW they do it, before finally getting to WHAT it is they do. Answering WHY gets to the emotional centre of the human brain, the limbic system, which is responsible for our emotions and has nothing to do with logic. As a result, your WHY should elicit some kind of emotional response in someone. Your goal as an artist, as is the goal for anyone running any kind of business, is to inspire people to action. This is the corner stone of marketing and something you should never forget. The trouble is, as an artist, the process of inspiring people to action isn't always a clear one.

Let's look at some examples.

Case Study: Disney's Magic Kingdom

It's no secret that one of my favourite companies is The Walt Disney Company. So of course I love Disneyland, which is the Anaheim, California version of The Magic Kingdom in Florida. But let's say that you live in a cave somewhere, have never heard of Disney, and know nothing about The Magic Kingdom. You poor soul! To put the importance of understanding your WHY into perspective, I want to show you how Disney has mastered this process, and, as a result, seen tremendous success with many aspects of its business, in particular its theme parks.

In 2006, a one-day ticket to Disney's Magic Kingdom in Florida would've cost you as much as $67.00. According to the Themed Entertainment Associations' annual Theme Park Attendance Report, the Magic Kingdom sold 16,640,000 tickets that year. But Disneyland has always battled complaints from its Guests that the lines are too long, the park is overcrowded, and therefore park Guests weren't having the best possible experience. To fix this, Disneyland has had to gradually raise its prices every year in an effort to meet the high demand, sell less tickets annually, and create a better park experience. In economics this is referred to as the law of supply and demand. But has it worked?

In 2017, Disney increased its prices for tickets to Florida's Magic Kingdom by 85 percent over 2006's prices. As a result, a one-day ticket would cost as much as was $124.00. Despite this, the Magic Kingdom actually sold 23 percent more tickets during 2017 - 20,450,000 according to TEA! WHY in the world is that happening? Simon Sinek would tell you that "it's because people don't buy what you do, they buy WHY you do it".

Of course there are many other amusement parks and theme parks around and they all more or less have the same list of offerings - food, rides or attractions, merchandise, and so on. So how would the creator of some of the greatest animated films of all time be able to convince the public that The Magic Kingdom should be chosen over the others? To tell you about Disneyland, the company could say "Disneyland is a theme park. It has great food and fun rides. Come to Disneyland!". But ask yourself this: does that inspire you to spend your hard earned money and valuable time to visit Disneyland over, say, Universal Studios? Does it give you a good sense as to why you would want to go to Disneyland instead of any other amusement or theme park? Probably not. Instead, Disney starts with WHY. In doing so the company has avoided the risk of simply blending in to an already crowded field of amusement parks.

At the opening of Disneyland in Anaheim, California in 1955, Walt Disney gave a speech that I would surmise is the WHY for all of Disney's theme parks and attractions around the world today. The speech was so inspiring, that the company had it memorialised on a plaque you can find at the park. When Disney gave this speech, he didn't want to tell you WHAT Disneyland is. He wanted to tell

you WHY Disneyland is. He knew that if he could inspire you to action and get you into the park, then you would not only experience WHAT Disneyland was for yourself, but that his staff (part of his HOW) would make sure you had a magical experience. When you read this quote ask yourself, how does this quote make me feel? Ignore any logical thoughts you may have as you read it like the fact that Disneyland is not actually yours or any of the cheesy talk about hopes, dreams, and idealism. If we assume that you buy into the same beliefs and values that Disney refers to in his speech then we can also assume that you're going to be more likely to want to visit the park. This is Walt's WHY for Disneyland.

Ask yourself the following questions and be completely honest about your answers: Why do I want to do music? Why has this particular project come about, and why at this particular time? Why these songs? If your answer to the above questions is anything remotely related to "because I want to make a living from my music" or "I want to be famous" then you're not being true to yourself when answering the questions. Those answers are outcomes. Your WHY should explain the reasons you want to achieve those outcomes. As an artist, sometimes this kind of self-analysis doesn't come naturally. It make take some time to get at honest answers. Take all the time you need, even if it's weeks or months. I'll explain more about the importance of giving this the attention it deserves in subsequent chapters. Taking from my experience, let me give you a music-related example of how to honestly find your WHY, which I hope you find helpful in discovering your own.

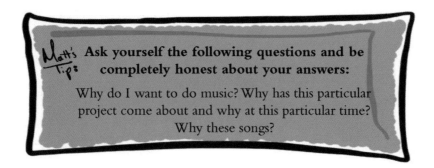

Matt's Tips: **Ask yourself the following questions and be completely honest about your answers:**

Why do I want to do music? Why has this particular project come about and why at this particular time? Why these songs?

Case Study: "Mirrors"

At the height of the excitement for my "Mirrors" album, I gave many print and radio interviews. I would inevitably be asked about the album, and I could've easily responded the typical way an artist responds:

Just Thought You Should Know

"The album is called 'Mirrors' and I got to work with a wonderful team and in the most beautiful studio. You can find it on iTunes and Amazon. I hope you enjoy it!"

This is a response similar to the ones I hear all the time (I'll give you an example later). I don't know about you, but a response like that doesn't inspire me to action. Remember that one of the most important things you have to do as an artist is to inspire people to act – whether you're trying to get them to want to buy your merch, sign up to your mailing list, or buy your music. If you can't inspire them to act, then you'll have a difficult time having a career in the music industry.

Instead, when someone asked me about the album my response was similar to this:

 I wanted to write an album about how I saw myself as opposed to how other people saw me, something that I think is a universal experience we all have at one time or another. In 2001 my cousin passed away after a long battle with Muscular Dystrophy, and he regularly battled this same problem with perception. Before he died at 15 years old, I promised him that after the release of my first big project I would donate some of the profits to the Muscular Dystrophy Association in his name. So now, $1 from every sale goes to MDA because no parent should every have to hear the words 'Muscular Dystrophy' again. And I got to work with wonderful songwriters and musicians for this project! The engineer and producer were incredible and I think we produced a project that all of us are quite proud of. I hope you enjoy the album!

Which response would make you more likely to go find your phone, open up your preferred streaming application, type in the artist's name (only to misspell it and have to look it up on Google), then go back to the streaming app and type it in again? I mean that's a fair amount of work, right? I'm guessing probably the second response. Hugh MacLeod, in his book *Ignore Everybody*, said, "Don't try to stand out from the crowd. Avoid the crowds altogether." You do this by understanding your WHY. Aside from this, understanding your WHY ahead of time also makes giving interviews a heck of a lot easier because you already know what you're going to say most of the time!

Case Study: Band A

Now let me give you an example of a band who went with the more typical response. I recently had this young band submit to be represented by Dreamscope. For privacy reasons, I'll refer to them as "Band A". Band A consists of three 20-something-year-old guys who have only been together as a group for a couple of years. Fortunately for them, they had quite a bit of cash to spend. So they rented out the famous Abbey Road Studios in London to record their single. They hired one of the most sought after PR agents here in London to keep them in the press. They had expensive PR photos taken, and they had produced a very high-end expensive music video for their single. In less than four months they had amassed 11,505 online views for the video, which was pretty respectable for a brand new band. I then saw that their PR agent had gotten them some great interview slots on big name TV shows in London. In one of them, the host asked the band to tell the audience about the single. Again, to protect their anonymity, I will paraphrase their response a bit.

Basically, their lead singer responded by saying he wrote the song about a girlfriend who had just broken up with him and whenever they performed it live people seemed to really like it so they made it their first single. Full stop. After hearing this, it became clear to me why Band A, after having spent loads of money on a fancy studio, on a high-end music video, high-end promotional photos, and after working with literally one of the best PR agents possible, had only 20 Spotify plays, 585 Instagram followers, 66 Twitter followers and 2,744 Facebook followers. Clearly something wasn't sticking, and all the money in the world wasn't going to fix it. Now they were sitting in front of me telling me they didn't achieve their definition of

19

success because they needed a manger to represent them. That's a load of crap.

The band didn't know their WHY, something only THEY could come up. Their team could support them in defining that WHY, but ultimately it had to come from them or else it would be inauthentic. Failing to clearly define their WHY had made them generic, and that was why all the money in the world couldn't deliver them the results they had hoped for. Instead of avoiding the crowd, they blended into the crowd with a canned answer and instantly became unremarkable. Remember: don't try to stand out from the crowd. Avoid the crowd altogether. Do this by being honest with yourself about WHY.

Develop Your Artist Brand

Just so you know, the odds are that you won't make a living selling music. There, I've said it. Get that in your head now, and get used to it. Your music is only one element of the greater brand that is your artist business. Developing this brand and business can be difficult, but if you've been honest about identifying your WHY, then you'll also be able to identify your likely target audience and effectively use your resources.

I remember seeing the show "Fantasmic!" at Disneyland for the first time when I was seven years old. After the show, I told my mom I wanted to be "that" Mickey Mouse one day because he was able to conquer evil and negativity with magic. Even at that age I wanted to make the world a more beautiful place, and it turns out that I'm able to do that through music. My WHY for my "Mirrors" album made me relatable. But then, after releasing the album, I received letters from solders in Iraq and Afghanistan and even from people fighting various ailments all over the world, which to me was a testament to the fact that I've been able to, in small ways, truly be that Mickey Mouse. I've even had messages from young people who have said that my music helped them avoid suicide. Now, eleven years later, I still get messages from people on a regular basis about how a song from that album helped them through something. How crazy is that? Somehow, through music, I have been able to be a part of the lives of so many people around the world, and I would argue it was because I had a clear understanding that the desire to inspire, to give hope, and to lead was at the very foundation of my art and work. In fact Dreamscope itself is based around teaching independent artists who are early in their careers how to be strong, independent musicians without getting screwed by people who should know better. The very culture I've created within Dreamscope is part of my "branding" as a creative person.

Let's apply the past to the present now. In preparing for my upcoming release, I have decided to use imagery and language that will more than likely connect with my current audience and, if done correctly, a new audience as well. While many of them stream, I know much of the audience who have followed me over the years still prefer a physical CD. I also know they want to connect with me personally, so I've packaged my release with physical items such as a physical copy of the album, handwritten lyrics, photographs and t-shirts, but I've also included more personal touches such as a phone call from me. In addition, I have a history of identifying great causes that I can relate to. With this project, I will be teaming up with organisations that help individuals in the LGBTQA community who have/ are experiencing domestic abuse because I believe it's not something we as a society think about when we think about domestic abuse, and it's something I've experienced myself. All of this fits nicely within my brand as an artist. Of course, as of the date of writing this, I am still in the planning stages. There will likely be changes to the plan as we go, but I hope that it gives you a clearer picture as to why it's important to understand your WHY before you can truly develop your brand.

Recently, I spoke with an artist who is very much into traveling. As she travels she does these great vlogs often featuring her meditation and spiritual aspects in addition to acoustic performances. I told her she was doing a great job of speaking to her audience and gave her the idea of creating her own brand of hand-made candles. I told her she could take it a step further by creating candles that have scents that remind her of certain places around the world she's visited. What do people who meditate like? Candles! Her music,

21

her candles, and her vlogs all tie into her a brand, and as these things develop she can expand on it even more.

Another artist I worked with is very into the new age movement. Her mother has roots in Eastern cultures, and the artist really identifies with them. She enjoys things such as meditation, poetry, using different stones that are supposed to enhance life in certain ways, psychics, etc. So I sent her away to think about things like what tastes, colours, sounds, behaviours, and ways of thinking people like her experience or gravitate towards. After much discussion, I pointed out to her that she could write a book of poetry where each section corresponds with one of the songs from her upcoming EP. Furthermore, the poetry could act as a sort of way to say the things she didn't have room to say on the EP. I told her that the e-book could also have the songs embedded in them at the beginning of each chapter. In the margins of the books she could even draw the cute crude drawings of rainbows and sunshine and stick figures that she enjoys creating so much.

You get the idea. After you have this, then, when you're about to release new music for instance, you can begin to develop fun product bundles. Suddenly you're not just selling your music. Next thing you know, you've got a concrete plan on how you can make money from your brand. Keep in mind that sometimes this takes artists years to get right. One of my friends who has been in the business for some 28 years only recently created a sister-website to her main artist website that promotes her beliefs on holistic living. Start small and allow it to develop as your career develops.

The Power of Motivations

In addition to having a clear idea of your WHY, I thought you should know some fundamental basics about what moves people to action, allowing your WHY to come to fruition. This has to do largely with motivations. Whether you're working with your artist team (which we'll get to in the next section) or simply want to understand how to better engage with your fans, having a grasp of the fundamental principles of human motivations is vital.

Think of a person's motivations as needs. Whether you realise it or not, the reasons you get up in the morning (or don't) and the reasons you make every single decision you do throughout your day is driven by your various motivations. No matter who you're working with, if you can quickly get an understanding of what factors are driving them, you'll naturally operate from a position of strength. Having a general understanding of motivations will also provide you with the tools you need to help find a solution that serves the needs of all parties involved. Although there are many books out there by individuals who study the topic for a living, I've decided to spend a bit of time on this section because I refer to it as my "secret weapon" in dealing with people.

Human Needs

We are all humans, and we obviously all have basic human needs. These needs can be a driving factor behind the decisions we make. Researchers have separated these needs into Primary needs and Secondary needs. Primary needs include everything you need to live: water, food, sleep, etc. Think survival. Secondary needs take into account a person's mind and spirit rather than their physical body. These can be particularly tricky. By nature, Secondary needs:

- Are strongly conditioned by experience
- Vary in type and intensity among people
- Are likely to change over time
- Cannot usually be isolated but rather work in combination and influence each other
- Are often hidden from conscious recognition
- Are vague feelings as opposed to specific physical needs
- Influence behaviour in powerful ways

Motivational Drives

To put it short, there are three main motivations behind what people do and the decisions they make. They can be driven by a desire to achieve (achievement motivation), a desire to relate to other people (affiliation motivation), or by their desire to influence people (power motivation). Of course, it's possible and totally normal that a person's singular decision or action can be driven by more than one of these. Although they are pretty self explanatory, lets take a look at each of them in a bit more detail.

People who are motivated by achievement like challenging goals. They are the ones that want to move up in the corporate ladder and they see accomplishments as the most important factor. They aren't so concerned with recognition or rewards, however, as they see advancement as recognition enough.

Affiliation motivation describes people who have a desire to relate to people on a social basis. They like to work with compatible people and feel best when experiencing a sense of community. As a result, the people they work with tend to become their closest friends and they love being noticed as having a good attitude and being very easy to work with.

Some individuals are driven by a need to influence others and this is called Power Motivation. These are the ones in groups who are quick to take charge and lead the team. They are eager to make an impact on their organisation and have no problem taking risks in order to do so.

Four Major Indicators of Motivation

Of course, you need to be able to tell if a person or a group is feeling motivated at all. Luckily, researchers have identified ways of doing this as well. The first way is through engagement which can be measured by noticing their level of enthusiasm, initiative and the amount of effort they put into an objective. Second, the degree to which the person or team acts as part of the team and how they are bonding will show commitment. Third, notice a person's level of satisfaction and experience of meaningful tasks. Finally, if you've got people leaving your team constantly then your turnover is bad and it could mean that you aren't motivating them very well.

Self-efficacy Affects Goal Setting

This refers to a person's internal thoughts about their job-related capabilities. It can be looked at either through a specific task or on the outcome of several tasks. People who have high self-efficacy usually have higher personal goals because they believe that they are attainable. It's important that, as the leader of your artist team, that you ensure that you help your team build self-efficacy. This can be done in several ways. Things like involving them in tasks and decisions, listening to their ideas, recognising their achievements, and talking to them with respect and not implying that they are stupid. All of this builds morale and make the team a more positive one to work on.

Study, Study, Study

I talked about this a bit in the first chapter, where I told you my story. When my Uncle Art told me to go and study, I was mortified. How boring! But actually it's not! In fact, I still study today. Maybe not always in the traditional sense of reading academic books and the like, but I am constantly reading about what other artists are doing, industry news, tech trends, and so on. I have developed a natural curiosity for all things related to music, and it has really helped me to be not only a better entertainer but also a smarter business person.

Studying performers as they perform a live concert is one of the most fun things to look at. I start by looking at the physical components of their signing. What shape did their mouth make when that particular note was hit, and how were they standing? Were their feet planted firmly on the ground? Was their neck stretched outward, or was their chin tilted downwards? If I found a note or register I wanted to emulate, I would try to make that same note in an octave comfortable for me. How did it feel? Did I push the sound to the back of my front teeth or was it largely held in in the back of my throat? Was I nasally? Then, of course, I look at their stage movements. How often do they move from one side of the stage to the other and is there any pattern to this? How often do they have breaks in between songs where the artist talks? When they do talk, what kinds of things do they say? Do they talk at the audience or do they bring the audience along on the journey with them? This is a never ending thing that I do as a performer and I know even instrumentalists who ask themselves as many, if not more, questions.

Studying other performers is such an easy and fun way to learn new things, and all the professionals do it.

Another thing I regularly study is industry trends. How are people consuming music? What is virtual reality doing to the way we experience concerts? There is now software that is programmed to write hit songs. What will this do to songwriters and is it likely going to take off? What kinds of things does this software think make a hit song? What are the current top markets in the world or in my country? What laws are being considered that will affect the industry and what exactly will that effect be? If you didn't know off the top of your head that the top 4 music markets around the world, according to the International Federation of the Phonographic Industry (IFPI), were the United States, Japan, the UK, and Germany, then you probably want to read up. If you didn't know that the United States is the largest music market in the world and has seen a 15 percent growth in revenue in 2018, then you might not be taken very serious as someone in the modern industry. This kind of information tells you what you should be doing as an artist. If your music isn't for sale in Japan, you might want to consider fixing that. What kind of music and artist does well in the Japanese market? The more you know, the easier it will be for you to make informed decisions about your career and you'll be taken more serious when you're in a room full of people in the industry because you're going to be seen as knowledgeable about the current industry trends.

This may sound like an odd thing to do as a musician, but I highly recommend taking acting classes. And make sure they include improvisation. You'll attend these lessons not to become a great actor, but to pick up some techniques. This will help you with things like timing stage movement, stage fright, being in the moment, and many others. If you're not comfortable taking acting classes, I would recommend the Masterclasses that the actors Natalie Portman and Samuel L. Jackson gives on the website masterclass.com. They are absolutely fantastic; however, they will not give you the same experience that attending acting classes would.

Finally, take music lessons. Vocalists should always take singing lessons. You might be able to carry a tune, but you might not be supporting yourself in the proper way of singing of breathing. Only a vocal coach can assess that and help you. Instrumentalist should also take lessons from other more experienced instrumentalists in an effort to better themselves.

I think one of the beautiful things about being an artist is the ability to take from the techniques and characteristics of other genres and adapting them into your own. For instance, as a result of that practice, I have a sound as a vocalist that may be reminiscent of certain other artists, but maybe only slightly. It has provided a richer and more unique experience for the listener and has added to my WHY as an artist.

Stay Focused

I know this may seem like another obvious pointer, but you wouldn't believe the number of times I thought this was clear only to find someone had derailed a bit and set the team back. Identify your goals early on, before bringing anyone onto you team, and then prepare yourself for achieving that goal by setting out rough ideas and plans. Then, after bringing your team on and giving them the direction do everything you can to keep everyone on message. All of the cogs in the clock need to be pushing the bigger cog in the same direction in order for the clock to keep working. You are the clock, and the bigger cog is the goal.

Just before signing her to Dreamscope, a young artist told us that her inspiration was Jesse J and that she wanted to emulate her with her project. She sent me images of what she wanted her promo photos to look like, all Jesse J, and told me that she wanted to explore more of her sensual side. Our A&R Manager was helping her to craft her songs in this kind of way and doing his best to teach her to be a stronger and more independent woman. This went on for months before it was time to have promo shots done for her. When I hired the photographer, I showed her samples of what the artist wanted and explained to her that we had our doubts that this was truly her but the artist was insisting that she was ready to show this side of herself. The photographer was game and excited to help the artist explore this side of her.

After the shoot was done, the photographer e-mailed me and said, "my vision was for her to be more 'fierce'! But she plays 'fun' much better in my opinion". Sure enough, the pictures were a lot less lioness and a lot more lion cub, and it didn't make for a great session because both the artist and the photographer were going for something that the artist wasn't ready for. The artist made no effort to prepare clothing that was particularly Jesse J-esque and she made no effort to communicate with the photographer beforehand.

Later, the artist complained that the photographer, whom we've used many times before and has always exceeded our expectations, wasn't good, which was why her photographs didn't come out the way she wanted. She then decided she wanted to have photographs that showed more of her Indo-Asian side, a direct contrast to what she had been telling us all along. As a result, her team was heading towards one goal, but the artist, herself, was floundering and didn't hold herself accountable for her misdirection and lack of proper planning. Remember the ideas, goals, and direction must come from your WHY and that will guide the activities of the people on your team and impact the tools used - your HOW.

DREAMSCOPE'S
★ARTIST
CHECKLIST

This is by no means a complete list and you should always consult with a lawyer, manager or even a mentor familiar with the music business. We cannot provide you with legal advice but we can guide you as you make some important first steps in your career!

☐ Register with a songwriter PRO

PRO STANDS FOR "PERFORMING RIGHTS ORGANISATION" AND AS A SONGWRITER, IT IS VITAL TO BE SURE YOU ARE REGISTERED. YOUR PRO PLAYS A BIG PART IN ENSURING THAT YOUR MUSIC IS PROTECTED AND THAT ANY MONIES OWED TO YOU AS THE SONGWRITER ARE INDEED COLLECTED AND PAID. IF YOU ARE IN THE UK, YOUR PRO IS PRS. GERMANY? GEMA. UNITED STATES? ASCAP, BMI OR SESAC.

☐ Draft an Agreement with your band

THIS STEP IS OFTEN OVERLOOKED CAUSING MANY PROBLEMS AMONG FRIENDS OR EVEN FAMILY. HAVING A BAND AGREEMENT SETS THE PARAMETERS FOR HOW THE BAND IS GOING TO OPERATE AND HOW DECISION ARE GOING TO BE MADE. SET THE GROUND WORK DOWN BEFORE YOU GET GOING SO EVERYONE IS CLEAR AND YOU'LL SAVE YOURSELF A LOT OF HEADACHES IN THE FUTURE.

☐ Buy your Artist domain

A DOMAIN IS ANOTHER TERM FOR YOUR WEBSITE ADDRESS. WWW.YOURNAME.COM IS IDEAL AND UNIVERSAL BUT THERE ARE MANY ALTERNATIVES. WHAT YOU DON'T WANT IS TO HAVE A HIT SONG AND THEN FIND THAT SOMEONE ELSE HAS BOUGHT THE DOMAIN CONTAINING YOUR NAME. THEY ARE CHEAP TO BUY (UNDER £20 A YEAR) AND IT'S VERY EASY TO DO SO THERE'S NO REASON NOT TO.

☐ Build your Artist website

WITH ALL OF THE OUT OF THE BOX SOLUTIONS AVAILABLE FOR VERY LOW COST OR FREE, THERE IS NO REASON NOT TO HAVE YOUR ARTIST WEBSITE. THIS SHOULD BE THE CENTRE POINT THAT ALL OF YOUR EXTERNAL PLATFORMS LINK TO AND FOR EVERYTHING ABOUT YOUR CAREER. KEEP IT FRESH AND UPDATED!

☐ Set up your Socials

'WEB PRESENCE' IS ONE OF THE MOST IMPORTANT THINGS YOU NEED TO HAVE TODAY. PEOPLE NEED TO FIND YOU! SOCIAL MEDIA HAS PROVIDED A GREAT TOOL FOR ARTISTS TO INTERACT WITH THEIR FANS DIRECTLY AND YOU SHOULD BE DOING IT! MAKE SURE YOU SET UP YOUR SOCIALS SEPARATE FROM YOUR PERSONAL ACCOUNTS USING PROFESSIONAL HANDLES. A GREAT EXAMPLE IS @YOURNAMEMUSIC OR ANY VARIATION. TRY TO GET THEM TO BE THE SAME ON ALL PLATFORMS.

☐ Demo Your Songs

DID YOU KNOW THAT YOU DO NOT NEED TO REGISTER YOUR MUSIC OR SONGS FOR THEM TO BE ELIGIBLE FOR COPYRIGHT PROTECTION? AS LONG AS YOU HAVE YOUR SONG "FIXED" - TYPED UP, NOTATED, DEMOED - THEN IT IS AUTOMATICALLY PROTECTED UNDER THE UK'S "COPYRIGHT, DESIGNS AND PATENTS ACT 1998". BEST OF ALL, THE "BERNE CONVENTION" AND "THE UNIVERSAL COPYRIGHT CONVENTION" ENSURES YOUR SONG IS ALSO PROTECTED IN NEARLY EVERY COUNTRY IN THE WORLD!

☐ Build your Web Presence

ALONG WITH HAVING YOUR ARTIST WEBSITE AND SOCIAL MEDIA CHANNELS, THERE ARE MANY OTHER PLATFORMS WHERE YOU CAN CREATE PROFILES THAT WILL ALLOW YOU TO BUILD YOUR WEB PRESENCE. VARIOUS FORMS OF ELECTRONIC PRESS KITS, MERCHANDISE STORES, TOUR PROMOTION OR BOOKING PLATFORMS, PHOTO GALLERIES AND MORE WILL ONLY HELP TO ADD TO THE NUMBER OF "HITS" YOUR NAME RECEIVES WHEN IT'S PUT INTO GOOGLE. THIS ENSURES THAT PEOPLE ARE ABLE TO FIND YOU EASIER AND QUICKER!

★ARTIST
CHECKLIST

☐ Choose a Distributor

AS A NEW ARTIST, YOU WILL MOST LIKELY USE ONE OF THE MANY MUSIC AGGREGATORS FOUND ONLINE SUCH AS CDBABY OR TUNECORE. THESE ARE A GREAT WAY TO GET YOUR MUSIC SOLD SO THAT YOU CAN EVENTUALLY DRAW THE ATTENTION OF A DISTRIBUTOR WHO WILL WORK WITH YOU TO INCREASE YOUR SALES. CHOOSE YOUR AGGREGATOR WISELY - SOME CHARGE UPFRONT FEES, SOME TAKE A PERCENTAGE OF SALES - THERE IS NO RIGHT OR WRONG WAY.

☐ Join Membership Organisations

THERE ARE MANY ORGANISATIONS AVAILABLE TO YOU AS A SONGWRITER, PERFORMER, COPYRIGHT OWNER, ETC. THESE ORGANISATIONS WILL OFTEN HOLD EVENTS FOR NETWORKING AND CAN PROVIDE A WEALTH OF VALUABLE INFORMATION TO YOU TO HELP GUIDE YOUR CAREER. THE BOTTOM LINE - GET INVOLVED IN YOUR MUSIC COMMUNITY! IT MAKES YOU LOOK MUCH MORE PROFESSIONAL, TOO!

☐ Keep track of that Metadata

IN AN INCREASINGLY DIGITAL WORLD, METADATA IS BECOMING MORE AND MORE IMPORTANT! METADATA - INFORMATION STORED WITHIN AN AUDIO RECORDING THAT IDENTIFIES THINGS SUCH AS THE ARTIST, LABEL, COPYRIGHT OWNERSHIP, AND MORE - ARE USED BY RADIO STATIONS, PROS, AND MANY OTHER ORGANISATIONS TO ENSURE YOU GET PAID. FURTHERMORE, WITH THE INCREASED USAGE OF SMART SPEAKERS, LISTENERS WANT TO BE ABLE TO FIND OUT WHO THE DRUMMER IN THAT SONG IS WHEN THEY ASK THEIR SMART SPEAKER. ITS ALL IN THE METADATA. USE A SIMPLE SPREADSHEET OR ONE OF THE MANY ONLINE TOOLS AVAILABLE TO HELP YOU KEEP TRACK.

☐ Get Insurance

WHETHER YOU'RE ON THE ROAD TOURING, IN THE STUDIO RECORDING, OR TEACHING A LESSON, YOU WANT TO MAKE SURE THAT YOU ARE PROTECTED FROM ACCIDENTAL DAMAGE, LOSS AND ANY LIABILITY. BEST OF ALL - IT'S CHEAP IN COMPARISON TO WHAT YOU COULD PAY FOR REPLACING DAMAGED GEAR. SOME ORGANISATIONS SUCH AS THE UK'S MUSICIANS UNION WILL AUTOMATICALLY INSURE YOU.

☐ Set up as a Limited Company

ALTHOUGH NOT ALWAYS REQUIRED, THERE ARE MANY POSITIVE REASONS TO SET YOURSELF UP AS A LIMITED COMPANY, ESPECIALLY IF YOU ARE BAND, AND IT'S EASIER TO DO THAN YOU'D THINK. AS A LIMITED COMPANY, YOU MAY BE PROTECTED (OR "LIMITED"), PERSONALLY, FROM VARIOUS LEGAL AND FINANCIAL SITUATIONS THAT MAY ARISE. IT'S ALSO A GREAT WAY TO KEEP YOUR PERSONAL AND PROFESSIONAL LIFE SEPARATE.

☐ Register as a Recording Copyright Owner

IF YOU HAVE PERFORMED ON AND/OR ARE THE OWNER/PARTIAL OWNER OF A SOUND RECORDING, THEN YOU ARE OWED A ROYALTY FROM ANYONE WHO PUBLIC PLAYS THAT RECORDING. IF YOU ARE IN THE UNITED STATES, YOU SHOULD REGISTER WITH SOUNDEXCHANGE. IF YOU ARE IN THE UNITED KINGDOM, YOU SHOULD REGISTER WITH PPL UK.

☐ Trademark your name or logo

AS A BAND OR SOLO ARTIST, YOUR NAME IS YOUR BRAND AND YOUR BUSINESS SO YOU WANT TO MAKE SURE THAT ONLY YOU CAN USE IT. TRADEMARK IS A GREAT WAY TO PROVIDE YOU WITH THAT PROTECTION. CHECK WITH YOUR LOCAL TRADEMARK OFFICE FOR DETAILS ON HOW TO REGISTER. USUALLY, IT CAN BE DONE ONLINE AND YOU CAN REGISTER IN ONE OR SEVERAL DIFFERENT "CLASSES" THAT COVER ACTIVITIES SUCH AS LIVE PERFORMANCE, SOUND RECORDINGS, MERCHANDISE, ETC. IT CAN BE QUITE COSTLY BUT YOUR NAME IS YOUR FIRST ASSET AND IT DESERVES PROTECTING!

☐ Build Your Team

IT'S GREAT TO LEARN ABOUT AS MUCH OF THE BUSINESS AS YOU CAN BUT THE BOTTOM LINE IS YOU WILL NEVER BE ABLE TO DO IT ALL ALONE. YOU NEED A TEAM. ARTIST MANAGER, PERSONAL MANAGER, LAWYER, ACCOUNTANT, RECORD PRODUCER, AUDIO ENGINEER, MUSICIANS, TOUR MANAGER, MARKETING AGENT, PR AGENT AND CO-WRITERS ARE ALL EXAMPLES OF ROLES THAT YOU MAY NEED TO FILL. MANY OF THE DUTIES THESE PEOPLE DO CAN BE MANAGED ON YOUR OWN BUT MANY OF THEM ALSO REQUIRE A GREAT DEAL OF TIME AND YEARS OF EXPERIENCE. FREE YOURSELF UP AS MUCH AS POSSIBLE TO CREATE AND DON'T TRY TO DO EVERYTHING ON YOUR OWN!

☐ Stay on top of the industry

THE MUSIC INDUSTRY IS CONSTANTLY CHANGING. IF YOU DON'T GROW WITH IT THEN YOU WILL BECOME IRRELEVANT. SUBSCRIBE TO YOUR LOCAL MUSIC BUSINESS TRADE MAGAZINE SUCH AS BILLBOARD IN THE UNITED STATES OR MUSICWEEK IN THE UK. ADDITIONALLY, MAKE SURE YOU EQUIP YOURSELF WITH MUSIC BUSINESS BOOKS FOR REFERENCE. YOU WILL USE THEM!

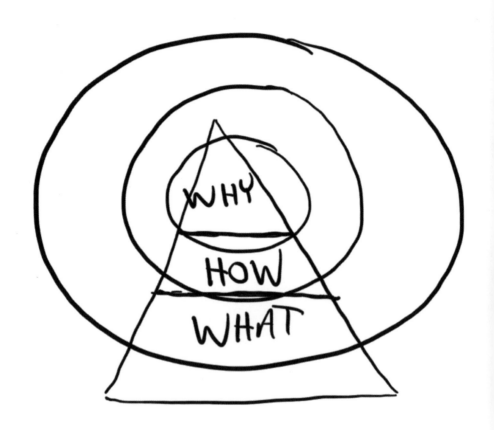

31

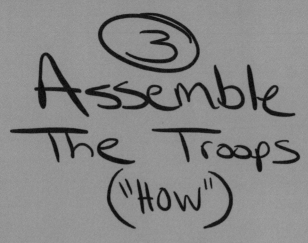

3
Assemble The Troops ("HOW")

YOU are a Business. Get Over It!

The earlier on you recognise this the easier it's going to be for you to achieve your definition of success. Whether you're a solo artist or a band, you are a business, and your first product is usually your music. Various kinds of merch are usually the next to be added to your product line, but it doesn't have to end here. As you progress in exploring your WHY, or as your WHY evolves, you'll find there are many other kinds of products or services you can offer as part of your artist business (go back and read the "Developing Your Artist Brand" section).

But as you are a business, your goal should be making money from your business. This means understanding your time is worth something. Your art has value, and if people want you to keep doing it, then they should come to expect there's a fee for accessing it. Yes, there will be times when it's necessary or beneficial to the long game for you to play the whole "we can't pay, but it'll be great exposure" game but do this sparingly. Maybe you want to test out new songs or you just want to get practice performing live. Then take advantage of being paid in exposure. But don't make a habit out of it. If another business is putting on an event or wanting to bring people in to a particular venue and they believe good music will be beneficial to this, then they should be willing to pay you. If more new artists understood their value, less of them would be taken advantage of. You are running a business. Just so you know, it is okay to ask for a fee. Demand it, even!

Register Your Online Domain

An example of an online domain is www.yourband.com or any of the variations of this you may want. This domain will point to the place your website is hosted or stored. It's important you own one or several domains. For instance, I own www.annecharico.com, www.mattannecharico.com but because I recognise it isn't necessarily simple to know how to spell my last name, I also own the domain www.officialmatt.com. All of them point to the same website. Best of all, they're not that expensive to own. The most common place people go for buying domains is Godaddy.com. Important note: when you buy a domain, you are required to register an address with it. Use your P.O. Box because this address will be made public on whois.net, and anyone will be able to find it. Remember your artist or band name is often your first asset as a business, and this is one way to begin protecting it.

Trademark Your Logo or Name

Remember your name is often your first asset as an artist, and you need to protect it. One way of doing this is to trademark your name. A trademark isn't the same as a copyright. A copyright is given to things such as any original written work, photography, music, etc. A trademark is a symbol such as a logo and/or a name that is legally registered or established as being used to represent a product or a company. There is legal precedence for companies who have sued and won in order to stop other companies from using a name even though the name wasn't formally registered with a government authority. This can be done by proving the when and how a name was first used in commerce. However, a for sure way of protecting your name is to just simply get it trademarked with your government. It can be a tedious process but it can also be worth it. Many record labels will trademark the artists' name straightaway but of course this means that the record label literally owns the artist. Don't let this happen. Do it yourself. You can find the details of your local trademark office by doing a simple search online.

Agreements

There are a number of agreements you should have in your arsenal so that you're properly protecting your business and your business' assets. There have been cases where lawsuits have been filed by greedy people because suddenly a project or an artist becomes successful and they want in on the money. If a good agreement is made at the moment you engage people to work with you, then there isn't further legal ground for them to stand on. They might even be friends or family. As sad as it sounds, money makes good people go bad.

First, if you ever use a session musician, whether it's for a live performance or a recording, use a session musician's agreement that clearly states the project or event you're engaging them to work with you on, the details of the event or project, the intended use, their agreed-upon pay, and any other relevant terms. If your friend is going to film a music video for you, get a smiler kind of agreement. If you have actors or models in your music video or in your photos, have a model agreement for them. If you are using a manager, an agent, an engineer, or a producer, there should be an agreement in writing. If someone wants to use your song in a student film, you need to have a synchronisation agreement. I know it can be a buzz kill. But the last thing you want is to not be protected should something go wrong. Remember, you are a business, and your chief concern should always be protecting your assets and your reputation.

Band Partnership Agreement

I cannot stress how important this is. After forming a band, you immediately need to set up a band partnership agreement in writing. In the agreement you should decide, collectively, on things like the band name, who makes certain decisions and how the decision will be made (even it's split evenly among each other), what happens when someone wants to leave the band, how the band's assets are split up, etc. You really should not start working as a band until this is complete because it lays down all the foundations for how things are going to work, and it eliminates any ambiguity in the future. Trust me - do it.

Smoke and Mirrors

There is a whole lot of smoke and mirrors happening in the music industry right now as a result of this culture of fear that has cropped up since the Napster-lead piracy revolution hit in 1999, which I touch on in the section on 360 degree deals later. It has spawned a wave of companies that prey on new and inexperienced artists who want an easy way to 'fame' and created a fragmented music business landscape that makes it even more complicated for artists to navigate. It's deceitful and its disgusting so I think you should know about it.

Some of these companies started up to legitimately promote the interests of independent artists. I worked with many of these platforms for things such as distribution, gig booking, etc. They were an integral part of my success, to be honest. But as they got bigger they also got more greedy and began pandering to larger artists, decreasing the amount of support staff available to help with any queries, and raised their prices for us little folk to be able to work with them. Because, as you know, independent artists have plenty of money to go around. Years later I even saw several of these companies take out ads in the Grammy programme that is handed out to attendees of the award show as they arrive. It was clear who their target market had now become but they achieved whatever business growth and success on the backs of people like me - independent artists - and I felt that it was rotten.

As a way to entice you to spend money on their platforms many companies out there will tell you how they give you these pretty sales charts or graphs and make it seem as though this is some kind of an exclusive thing. Some will even tell you that they can get you sales data before anyone else. For certain digital stores this may be true if that a company has some kind of special deal with a particular store however for two of the biggest stores, Apple and Spotify, you can get this same exact data before any distributor or aggregator can and I'll talk more about this later in this chapter. You don't need them for this. To me, this is yet more proof that the industry doesn't understand artists today.

More smoke and mirrors that companies like to serve up is when they tell you that they will collect all your publishing royalties for you or that they will get your music in tv/films. Be very careful with this. Many companies offering to collect your publishing royalties for you are offering you whats called an Administration Deal, which we will talk more about later when we discuss publishing, and can often make things more difficult for you in the long run. Many of these companies utilise a software that allows them to digitally register your songs all around the world in an automated process that is one size fits all. They could have the software set up in such a way that it allows them to accommodate different circumstances you may have however their business models are set up in such a way where, if they can hire less staff and automate the process as much as possible, then they can potentially make more money. One company in particular will deal with co-writers for you however that co-writer has to also set up an account with them and pay their fee before they will even work with you. You might ask yourself "why am I paying you a fee to represent me as a publishing administrator?", which would be a fair question to ask. Due to their business model you can forget being able to contact anyone by phone or receiving a competent reply via email, which is based on my personal experience and the experiences of people on many public message boards. In short, they take your up-front fee, they take exclusive rights to your compositions, and then they aren't available when you need them to be. My advice, if you want a Publishing Administrator, is to work with a publisher that only deals with publishing and nothing else. But always take time to read the fine print and be very careful with any company you are looking to work with.

Another culprit of the usage of the ol' smoke and mirrors tactic is record labels, particularly smaller independent record labels. You would think they would be on our side because they are independent like you. Not always the case. I've been warning people in my circle about this for a long time and recently I had a friend send me over a contract he was offered from a small independent record label and it was a dirty contract that the company offered after using their smoke and mirrors tactic to rope him in. What these labels do is invest loads and loads of money into big beautiful fancy equipment, as if this is what is necessary in order to make a great recording anymore today, bring you into their studio and show you around, and then once you're blinded by the light they get you to sign on the doted line. But not so fast. These contracts can often be riddled with unreasonable terms, ownership of your material, fees, etc. But because you were blinded by the flashy gear, they are hoping you don't notice. Of course, since they are sleazy, they have made sure that their contract is iron clad by adding a common clause that says, by signing the contract, you are acknowledging that you've sought the advice of a qualified music lawyer. It's rotten but this is why you should always actually seek this kind of advice.

I think this all comes back to the old adage that if its too easy or seems too good to be true then it very well might be. These companies know you want to make money from your music. They know that, in some cases, you may crave fame and attention. They also know that you are very likely not going to understand the industry and will probably not seek the advice of someone who does know better than you. Please do not fall for this trap. Do not sign anything or pay anyone money until you've gotten advice from a qualified lawyer or someone who has legitimate experience in the industry. Again - I just thought you should know.

No, You Can't Do It Alone

News flash: you can't do it alone. The very fact that you are reading this now is confirmation of that. You will undoubtedly see, if you haven't already, many music companies trying to tell you otherwise. They will sell you on things like "be your own label" and offer you gimmicks and use smoke and mirrors to make you feel like you can, in fact, do it all yourself. You can't. And let's be real - they want your money so they are telling you what they think you want to hear. The fact is, yes, there are many things that you can do yourself. Ironically, many of the things that those companies pitch as exclusive offers are set up to make you think that only they can offer it to you when actually you can do it very easily on your own. The manner in which it's presented is quite often the only exclusive part about it and that really has no bearing on your artist business. They are preying on your naivety. I want to change that. You should make it a point to at least have a general understanding of all aspects of your artist business. If you want to have a long term career then you've got to treat it like a job and there are many applicants out there for that job so you better bring your A game, baby. But regardless of all of this you still need a team of people - yes, even a record label - in different ways than you would've had you been starting your career twenty-five years ago. It's disgusting that these companies prey on emerging artists, if you ask me, and you'd be wise to consider the motives of any company you may work with.

Continuing with the references from Simon Sinek's Golden Circle theory, we can put this theory into action by noticing that the circle corresponds with a typical company's hierarchal triangle. If we place this triangle over the top of the Golden Circle, we will find that the WHY corresponds with the space at the top of the triangle typically reserved for the company owner, the HOW corresponds with where management sits in the company hierarchy, and the WHAT is an

> **Everything starts with the artist and with the music, that's what opens the door and that's why it's important that everyone at the label has a close relationship with artists**
>
> - Eric Wong, COO at Island Records
>
> *Source: IFPI Global Music Report 2019

outcome. This is no accident. The WHY can only come from you, the artist and the owner of your artist business, and therefore it's you who sets the direction for your project, your career, etc. This is the reason I told Band A from the previous chapter that having a manager wasn't necessarily going to be of benefit to them. HOW you get there is the area where your artist team sits. They will be the ones who carry out the WHY that you've already more or less defined. They might recommend ways of improving that WHY but as I've said previously, ultimately, the WHY has to come from you to be authentic. Your team is a major part of your HOW albeit not the only part of your HOW.

So who is your team? That's largely going to depending on many factors, including things like your finances or what stage of your career you're currently in. Below is a comprehensive list (not a complete list) of who your team might be comprised of in more advanced stages of your career as an artist.

* **Personal Manager**
* **Business Manager**
* **Accountant**
* **Contract Lawyer**
* **Intellectual Property lawyer**
* **Social Media Manager**
* **Live Booking Agent**

* **TV/Film Agent**
* **Publisher**
* **Record Label**
* **Radio Plugger**
* **PR Manager**
* **Photographer**
* **Cinematographer**
* **Recording Engineer(s)**

* **Mixing Engineer(s)**
* **Mastering Engineer(s)**
* **Tour Manager**
* **Session Musicians**
* **Live Musicians**
* **Distributor**
* **Graphic Designer**
* **Arranger**

Of course, depending on what stage of your career you're in, one or two people and with hope yourself, will be involved in many of these areas rather than just one person for everything. That's totally normal. The point of this is to show you that behind every artist is some kind of team of very smart and creative people. The artist can't do it on his or her own.

Working With Your Team

This is where things can get a bit tricky. Anyone who tells you that working with a team is easy is lying. It can be one of the most difficult things you do as an artist. But if you learn to do it right, it can be the most rewarding - not just for you, but for everyone involved.   I have the perspective of working with a team as an artist myself. Since I started Dreamscope, I now have the perspective of what it's like from the other side, too. Below I've listed my top five tips on how to best work with your Artist

Team. It's taken me years to figure this stuff out, so I'm excited to share them with you now.

Remember that you chose your team. With hope you chose individuals you feel can help you to carry out your WHY. That means that until they give you a reason to feel otherwise, you need to trust them 100 percent. Even if they've given you a reason not to totally trust them any longer, you still need to analyse things like the communication that was used to see if maybe something could've been done better to get the results that you wanted. Whether it's a mixing engineer that you hired to mix your music or a manager that you hired to push your agenda, you need to understand that they (usually) want to make sure you're happy with their work. But there is also a bit of selfishness involved in that they are trying to better themselves, too. This is okay! In working with you, clearly they feel like they have something to offer to you but they also feel like they can better their current situation by working with you. Relationships are often transactional. So trust them unconditionally to do the job you hired them to do. I'm not talking about blind trust. You should never hesitate to ask questions and seek understanding. Personally, I love when the artists that I work with have questions about things because it shows engagement with the process and that is a key aspect of Dreamscope's philosophy.

Build a relationship with the members of the team. You don't have to become best friends. Sure, you might share some personal things with each other and you might go out for drinks or dinner occasionally. This bonding time is key for both of you. It can even help create a bit of cohesion for everything else. Of course members of your team are probably working for other artists, and you need to be okay with that, too. But creating some kind of a bond between you and the people on your team will simply make them want to work harder for you. Don't pass up the shot.

You teach others how you want to be treated. Admittedly, I think I borrowed that line from a Dr. Phil show, but it's so true. Stop whining about how people are treating you and take some ownership in your part of that process. If someone on your team honestly isn't giving you the kind of attention you need and you let it go because you'd rather avoid healthy conflict, then you're teaching that person that it's okay. If you look back on the interactions that you've had with someone on your team and you can honestly say that things such as the frequency of your catchups, the manner in which the person interacts with you, the sense of urgency they have when dealing with something for you, and so on, is not fair or sufficient, then it's up to you to have a conversation about it with them. Understand that this is totally okay. This is different than being a diva. Don't be a diva. It's what I referred to earlier as healthy conflict. If you don't have that conversation then, you don't get to complain about the issue later. So address problems and concerns directly and early. Part of respecting your team is giving them the opportunity to right a wrong.

Learn how to communicate effectively. Communication is a tricky beast. When done right, you actually don't need to use a lot of words because the other person just understands you. When done wrong, it can cause a mess and unnecessary stress on everyone. It's important to understand that communication is about what the receiver understands and not about the information that you're trying to send. That means that if you have said something to your team and they didn't respond in the manner in which you'd hoped, then you need to first analyse the way in which you communicated the message to find ways to improve it. You then need to find ways to communicate that works best for the other person. Some people prefer receiving information in e-mail. Some people prefer face-to-face talks. Some people prefer quick messages through a messaging platform. Find what works, and stick to it. At the same time, remember what I said in tip three about teaching others how you want to be treated. If there's way you prefer to receive information from your team, then you need to make your team aware of this so they know how to communicate effectively with you, too.

41

It's also worth noting that some information is better shared and received in person or via teleconferencing. Tone of voice, facial expressions, and body movements all play an important role in the message you are trying to send. Email or SMS can miss the mark in certain situations. Do not ever underestimate the power of vocal tone, facial expressions, and body movements. Often they can be more powerful than words.

Once you have all of that more or less ironed out, make sure to have open and frequent communication with your team. Do not try to sugar coat things. Do no tell half of the story, even if the whole story paints you in a bad light somehow. If you're open and honest with your team then any problems can be dealt with. That is why they are there. Remember that they are on your side. They are meant to guide your career, not control it. The moment anyone else starts to control your career then you need to be stepping in to remind them that it's your artist business they work for. Still, you need to trust the fact that they know what they are doing. This brings me to my final point.

It's important to communicate with your team in a respectful manner. Remember that anything they're doing is likely coming from a place of love and passion. If this isn't the case, you need to find someone else to be on your team. You have brought them onto your team because they have a certain skillset, have certain knowledge, and likely have certain connection that you think could benefit you. These people likely spent years of time and loads of money to acquire all of this. To the contrary, you likely don't have this extensive experience that they do in their area which is why you hired them in the first place. It's fine if you aren't sure about something that someone on your team has done, or you want to know more about it for your own development. You should communicate that to your team member in a non-threatening manner. If, afterwards, you decide that you aren't happy about something they've done, communicate as well to them in a way that's respectful and constructive.

Be Kind. I can't tell you how much work I've gotten not because I was necessarily the best person for the job - after all, there are so many amazing performers out there – but because I was respectful and kind in addition to being able to do the job well. In this business, kindness and respectfulness is such a rare commodity. Use that fact to your advantage.

A very talented A&R scout for a big indie label who was trying to sign me to their label has a personal website for his side endeavours in the music industry. On a section of his website containing external links, he had a link posted on my website with a caption that read, "Matt is one of the smartest, kindest, and easiest people to work with in the music industry". That's called free marketing. If you saw a review for a business that had that same line you'd more than likely be interested in working with that person. I am totally okay with that, and you should be, too!

Also remember that these people have personal lives and you may not know what they are going through all the time. It's great when we as humans are able to not let our personal life interfere with our professional life but remember that sometimes this will happen. This makes it even more vital to communicate with your team from a place of respect and kindness.

Let's Talk Record Labels

At some point, you will need a record label. It might be sooner than you think. The hard part isn't simply finding a record label that can help you realise your WHY, but also finding one that truly understand what it means to be a record label in 2019. Regardless, a record label's job is to invest you their artists in various ways. It's a business proposition. It's not fair for an artist to come to a record label with the idea of "what can you do for me." Odds are you will more than likely not get a reply if you take this approach. You have to come from a "here's how I believe we can work together, and here's the value I can add to your company."

When to Look For a Record Label

Truth be told, this is going to change from record label to record label depending on their prerogatives. In general, a record label isn't going to be interested in working with you until you've shown that you've done a bit of leg work yourself, and rightfully so. As I mentioned before, a record label's job is to invest in you; a label isn't going to want to invest in someone who hasn't also invested in themselves.

That being said, it isn't always the case. Dreamscope doesn't see the listener as its primary customer. The artist is. So when we offer an artist a contract, we look at what they've been doing for themselves, just like any record label would. But we also consider the person. Since the deal is an artist development deal (more on that in a moment), having little to no experience isn't necessarily a reason we would turn someone down. We take a very non-traditional approach to being a record label in that I don't want to offer a traditional record contract. Dreamscope offers an artist development and production contract in which the recording is simply part of the artist's development process. This is incredibly unique and is much more akin to what's known in the industry as a service deal. Nick Cave's manager, Brian, once said in an interview that "there's no reason why service deals can't be a structure that works for emerging artists. The thing with most young developing talent is that it takes a long time to develop a career. That sits outside of whether someone's got a record deal, a label services deal, or self-releases. There's no technical reason why it can't happen...it's clearly just super-risky and tough to raise finance for young developing artists."

At the time of writing this, I personally have not come across a record label that takes the same approach that Dreamscope. Most record labels want to see a virtually finished 'product' before they consider working with you. This includes great promotional photos, great recordings, maybe a great music video, a large fan base, and so on. It really comes down to the type of deal you're being offered. I would argue that in deciding to look for a record label you have to also know what kind of record deal you want to be signed to.

Since the goal of this book is to give you a more holistic approach to your career, I'm going to only briefly talk about the most common types of recording deals out there today. For a more in-depth look at recording deals, I would highly recommend checking out Ann Harrison's book *Music: The Business.*

360 Degree Record Deal

In the late 1990s the music industry was screwed over by internet piracy and file sharing. As a result, profits plummeted from all-time highs in 1999, and the recorded music industry panicked. As a way to help combat this, services like iTunes popped up and offered record labels a platform to legally sell digital downloads to customers. The problem for the recording industry is that these platforms insisted that it would have to be at a price that listeners, who might otherwise turn to piracy, would be willing to pay. Lower, basically, than what the industry was used to. But some income was better than none. Once they finally agreed, record labels had to come up with other ways of making money since their profits from recordings would still be taking a hit. Insert the 360° Deal.

Put in the easiest terms, with a 360° Deal, the record label is able to take profits from the artist's other entertainment-related income. The mindset being that "you need us and without us you can't make much money as a creative person". This means that concert ticket sales, merchandise sales, acting opportunities or other tv/film appearances you make, books you write, modelling opportunities, brand sponsorships, and so on are all on the table for the record label to take a sizeable cut from. These deals are more or less the new industry standard and leave the artist, particularly a new artist but larger ones as well, with a very small cut in royalties, usually under 15 percent. In addition the record label will maintain ownership of the master recording for the life of copyright. They will lock you into a long term deal stipulated usually by the number of projects you must release before you are able to leave the contract but sometimes stipulated by a certain number of years. Lastly, they will likely want control of your branding and creative control over your career.

In my opinion, this deal was reactionary to the climate in society at the time. It wasn't forward thinking in the way the industry had the chance to be. In short, they panicked. Ever since this time period, the recorded music industry has been playing the victim instead of focusing on adapting to the demands of the consumer and, as the 2000s progressed, the needs of artists as well. Even today they still want to hang on to an archaic model that just simply does not work anymore because artists do no need record labels in the same way they once did, and consumers are increasingly changing the way in which they access recorded music. For better or for worse, the recorded music industry relies on the 360° Deal as its way of surviving today.

Project-specific Deals

Many smaller record labels are offering deals that are for a particular project only. Whether such a deal is for a single, an EP, or an entire album, it can be a great way for an artist to work with a record label on a very limited basis. In general, though, many of these deals take from the 360° model in terms of the splits and ownership of the material, but because they are project-specific, you generally won't lose control over your brand or lose money from other aspects of your career.

Production Deals

This is the most typical form of project-specific deal and also the most desirable if you don't want to sign with a record label. These deals are usually offered by a person with expertise in sound engineering and access to recording faculties who are trying to make a living themselves or sometimes can be financed by larger companies as a way to source talent. Like any other project-specific deal, they are generally geared for artists who are at early stages of their careers. Since they are low risk to the record company or the individual, there's typically no investment made into your career other than maybe a bit of word-of-mouth marketing. However, unlike other project-specific deals in general, the rights, risk, and royalties are split 50-50.

Why You NEED a Record Label

If you're reading this book, odds are you're at the early stages of your career. While there's a lot you can do on your own today thanks to technology, you're still going to want to be affiliated with a record label at some point. What isn't explained very well by the industry and what is certainly not represented by deals like a 360° Deal, is why you still need a record label.

Back in the day, a record label was your gateway to recording facilities as well as to audio engineers, mixing engineers, radio pluggers, marketing representatives, and so on. Let's face it people, today you don't need record labels for those things. You are able to make a record on your own and distribute it to the world for next to nothing. Of course you might be sacrificing quality unless you know how to properly record and mix your music, which, again, many of you know how to do. Thanks to the internet, as we will talk about in the marketing section, you are able to do a great deal of your own marketing as well. So why DO you need a record label today?

The truth is record labels still play a vital role in the careers of new artists. Record labels invest a lot of money into the careers of emerging artists, much of which is never recouped. They possess a pool of talented and well-connected individuals who are eager to do what it takes to make an act a success. They have the know-how and knowledge you need, and in many ways are still gatekeepers to the industry despite their diminishing role.

Of course, I would argue that record labels still have it all wrong. They are still playing the poor-me card. If the industry really wants to see growth again, it needs to change its mindset into one that recognises its role is to act in service to the artists, rather than to own the artist. The artist should be seen as a partner or even an employee. Likewise, the listener is not an adversary; they too are a partner. But thanks to things like social media, it's up to the artist to take the lead on engaging with the listener, while the record label is more or less there for support.

Contacting a Record Label

Dreamscope receives artist submissions, and, honestly, we love them! I'd like to think that all labels do, but I know for a fact it's not the case. Many labels prefer to find you rather than for you to find them, but I think this is part of the backwards thinking that simply must change in order to create a better environment within the industry. I've noticed that when artists submit to Dreamscope, there are certain things they all say, in one form or another. I have compiled a mental note of some of the things that are an automatic turn off. Please do not say these things. Remember that you're making a business proposition to a potential partner in your career. It cannot be all about "what can you offer me". There has to be a little bit of "what I can offer you". Right – here's my list of no-nos:

1. **"...have garnered great attention from critics"**. When I read this I just assume that you are talking about your mother because if music critics are paying attention to you then you probably have labels also paying attention to you and you wouldn't be emailing me.

2. **"I need help to be launched to my rightful place in the music industry"**. You don't want my response to this statement. It's not nice. Unfortunately I hear phrases like this a lot. Just…don't.

3. **"Let me know what you think"**. Umm….why should I? Being told to do this or even asked to do this will not make me want to do it. Give me a reason to want to give you this information but don't bother asking or telling me to.

4. **"I'm looking to take my career to the next level"**. You and literally every new artist out there. What does this even mean, anyway? 'Next level' is different for everyone. You can just leave this phrase or any variation of it out of your email, please.

5. **"I have a producer"**. This is a big one for UK artists, for some reason. As if a producer is somehow the music career magicians in and of themselves. No. As amazing as it is to have a great music producer on your side, they are only a small part of your team. It's unnecessary to say this at all.

6. **"Let me know how you can help me"**. Again, you're making a business proposition. The difference is, you know, more or less, what a record label does but the record label knows nothing about you. Instead, try something along the lines of "I'd like to learn more about your label and find a way that we might be able to work together".

I can't speak for other labels but I'm much more interested in things like why you want to be in the industry, why you are contacting my label specifically, what you've been doing for yourself, why you think you and Dreamscope can work well together. Many of the e-mails I see are generic, and it doesn't make me want to invest in that artist. Remember that a label's main job is not to record and distribute music anymore. It's to develop and invest in an artist. That being said - why would I want to invest in you? That question so far is very rarely ever answered. Tell me your WHY.

Let's Talk Digital Distribution

What's most important for you to know about distributors is there are two different methods of digital distribution. There are aggregators, and there are distributors, and they are not the same even though they ultimately accomplish the same thing. You have to decide which method is best for you. From there you can decide which company you are most interested in being affiliated with. Choose wisely, though. Examine all of the small print and ask as many questions as you have before you commit because once you commit then it can be a pain to move everything to a different company. Before we get to the two kinds of digital distribution methods, it's good to go over some terminology.

UPC and ISRC

Every product for sale to the public carries a Universal Product Code, or UPC, attached to it for tracking purposes. Usually there's a corresponding barcode made especially for a specific UPC to allow computers to easily and digitally identify the product. Every body of work (album, EP, single, and so on) that you release must have a UPC code. If you need a barcode for the UPC there are several free barcode generators online that can be found just by searching the web.

Similarly, an International Standard Recording Code, or an ISRC, is assigned to each track on a release to allow for the tracking and usage of a song. The code along with other pieces of information about the recording and the song are embedded into the song by the aggregator. Let's imagine that you have a ten track body of work that you're ready to release. Then means that you'll need a UPC for the album itself and an ISRC for each track on that album. If you are releasing a single then you'll have a UPC for the single and an ISRC for the song. It's very important that every time the song is released in a new way, whether it be a different edit, a remix, or as part of a different body of work, that it is assigned a new ISRC. So if you are releasing a single from your upcoming album you'll have two bodies of work: the single and the album. Each body of work will have its own UPC. but the recording as it appears on the single and the same recording as it appears on the album must have separate ISRC.

Digital Aggregator

An aggregator is someone who will distribute for absolutely anyone. Most musicians who are just starting out use an aggregator. Examples are TuneCore, CDBaby, and Distrokid. These companies sometimes operate on a commission of sales or by yearly fee. Now as there are so many digital aggregators out there these companies are being forced to build partnerships with other businesses in an effort to offer additional perks to their packages. When you distribute using an aggregator, they will all, however, assign UPC codes, ISRC codes, provide detailed sales reporting, and allow you to choose the store(s) you'd like to distribute to.

TuneCore

TuneCore was founded in 2005. Frank Black, the lead singer of the Pixies, was the first to use its distribution services. In 2015, the company was acquired by Believe Digital, which allowed it to greatly expand what it offers to artists, including distribution to more than 150 stores in 200 countries, Publishing Administration, and a whole catalogue of Artist Services. Signing up for an account is free, and you don't pay for anything until you're ready to distribute a project. At the time of this writing, you can distribute an album for $29.99 USD and a single for $9.99 USD in the first year. Every year after you pay a maintenance fee of $49.99 USD every year for an album and $9.99 USD for a single. TuneCore does not take a cut from your sales. You simply pay the yearly maintenance fee.

CDBaby

CDBaby is the world's oldest and largest distributor of independent music. The company has been around since 1998, first offering physical distribution to artists. Today, they are owned by Downtown and offer very similar services as TuneCore, it's closest competitor. The biggest difference between TuneCore and CDBaby is that CDBaby offers tiered accounts and no annual pricing. Under the standard CDBaby account, distribution of an album will cost you a one-time fee of $49 USD and a single will cost you $9.95 USD. Their pro tier, which offers all of the same services as the standard service in addition to registering the songs you've written with performing rights organisations worldwide like ASCAP and PRS, will cost you a one-time fee of $89 USD per album and $34.95 USD per single. CDBaby will continue making money by keeping 9 percent of your sales revenue instead of charging an annual fee like TuneCore.

Distrokid

As of writing this, Distrokid remains my personal favourite aggregator. The company formed in 2013 and offers to distribute your music to more than 150 stores worldwide quicker than any other aggregator for a percent of your royalties. Again, like most digital aggregator they offer a host of artist services through its partners and through additional services that it has established and you'll be able to download sales reports. What is unique about Distrokid, however, is the ability to set up splits with your collaborators which means that anyone you work with on a track can automatically get a percentage of sales instead of you having to do it yourself. As the company grows I anticipate they will need to up their fees or start taking a small percentage of sales in order to be sustainable. Either way, watch these guys. They are on to something good.

Traditional Distributors

Traditional music distributors offer a lot of the same artist services and reporting that an aggregator does. The difference is a traditional distributor will always take a commission and therefore will only want to work with

51

you if they believe they can make money by distributing your work whereas an aggregator will work with anyone and there's no approval processes. Some distributors only distribute in specific territories because that is where they have the best relationships with the industry. Having a distributor is ideal because usually you are given an account manager who looks after your music and if you've got a particularly big release the distributor may decide to do their own marketing because they stand to make more money if the project does well. As an emerging artist, you're more likely to use an aggregator, and that's okay. But make it a goal to work hard enough to be an attractive client to potential distributors in the future.

Let's Talk Marketing Tools

Your HOW is more than the people on your team. Your HOW is also about the tools you or your team uses to achieve your goals. There are a lot of things you need to consider and get set up before you begin a marketing campaign or do any marketing at all. Remember that marketing is a two-sided coin. One side is about promoting yourself, while the other side is about understanding who to promote to by knowing who is paying attention.

During a music business training I was giving to one of Dreamscope's artists about marketing, she stopped me and in a frustrated tone of voice said, "how can I talk about marketing when we haven't even gotten my final mixes done yet? It's like a cake shop with no cake in the windows!" This told me straightaway that she hadn't done the proper thinking about her WHY. She seemed to think that she needed her final mixes back to influence her marketing instead of understanding that her music and her marketing are two separate pillars that are working together to hold up her WHY.

I asked the artist to stop for a moment and think about what it took to make that cake shop that she mentioned. Before they opened their doors they had to research and test suppliers, they needed graphic designers, marketing guidance, equipment, materials, some kind of accounting system, maybe even a lawyer or two, and so on. All of this before they could even consider putting cake in the windows and opening the doors. The cake is the outcome - the WHAT - and logic says that you cannot have the outcome before thorough preparation, planning, and hard work. Just like everyone knows to expect to be able to buy cakes from a "coming soon" cake shop, they also expect to buy new music from a "coming soon" artist. What people really want to know is why you're different from everyone else that sells cakes or releases music. You can't have WHAT before WHY if you're going to be successful.

This section is going to get pretty intense. Take your time and try not to get overwhelmed. It's also worth noting that the recommended resources here are definitely not a definitive list. There are so many similar resources you can find simply by searching. The key to this document is to teach you what to search for. Lastly, as you will be (should be) collecting data, it's important to understand the data laws in your part of the world to ensure you're complying.

Connect With Your Audience

I don't mean try to talk to them all. But then maybe I do. In your research, have you found that your audience is likely to be on their mobile devices or are they more likely to be at a computer? Do they have an affinity for one music streaming or downloading platform or the other? Are there certain words or phrases that you want to use that your audience really identifies with? What imagery will they identify with? Do they like videos over pictures? If so, will they be more likely to watch a 15 second video or can you keep their attention for a full, three-minute video? What other artists or bands do they like? What do they do in their spare time? What books do they read? What shows or movies do they watch? Are they into technology or do they tend to be old school? Are they progressive or conservative in how they think? What part(s) of the world are they from and how might that shape their lifestyle? Are they religious? Do they like fast food or are they into health and fitness?

You get the point. That's what I mean by connecting with your audience. Who are they? That will tell you exactly what you need to do with every aspect of your marketing.

The Importance of Analytics

As an online "business", analytics tools are paramount. This data collection allows you to understand things like what social media posts people are reacting to the most, the content people seem to be most interested in, how/where/when they access your content, as well as age, gender, geo location, and more. This is important because once you can understand what makes your audience tick then you can continue to give them more of what they want, when they want it and in the manner in which they want it. This, of course, increases your fan base and grows sales. But if you don't have it set up to begin collecting this data then it is going to be very difficult for you to understand what works and maybe more importantly - what doesn't work. A great book to read on this is called *The Tipping Point* by Malcolm Gladwell. Check it out.

Let's take a look at the different ways that you can obtain and manage your artist business' analytics data.

Facebook Pixels and Google Tracking IDs

Facebook and Google have created some of the most powerful analytics tools out there. When you set up your accounts with them, you will be able to generate Facebook Pixels and Google Tracking IDs that are hidden on your website, in your links, or on other external websites to help you better understand the behaviours of people who interact with these assets. A warning: this can get really complicated really fast. You can track so many different behaviours and activities but I'm going to keep it to tracking just the basics for the sake of this discussion.

For Facebook, you'll need to create a profile on Facebook's Business Manager. In order for you to do this you need to first have a business Page set up (your artist Page, not your personal profile) and, if you want to include data from Instagram, your artist Instagram account should be set up as a "business" as well. If your Instagram isn't set up as a business (go do it now), it can be done easily in the settings of your Instagram account. Once you have these two things, you can simply go to business.facebook.com and set up your Business Manager. During the setup, Facebook will ask for your business name. Just use your name for this.

Once your Facebook Business Manager has been created, you can go into the "Business Settings" and add any Pages you manage as well as any Facebook Ad Accounts and Instagram accounts you have. Odds are, you will have a different Facebook Ad Account assigned to each Page you run which is smart for keeping things separate and also because you may choose to work with certain people or partners who would want to contribute to an ad campaign for you. You probably only want to add a partner to an ad account associated with a Page that is relevant to that partner. If you don't have an ad account set up, don't worry. But it is something you should set up soon because you should run Facebook ads at some point to drive people to your website or to your music. We will talk more about Ad Campaigns later. All of this, including adding partners and people to help manage your Page and Ad Accounts, can be done through Business Settings.

The Tools section of Facebook's Business Manager is where you'll be able to create Facebook Pixels, which allow you to track activity on non-Facebook platforms (like websites). For instance, I have my main domain, www.officialmatt.com, which points to a website that I host on Wix. The website has its own Facebook Pixel and Google Tracking ID. However, the other two domains that I own, www.annecharico.com and www.mattannecharico.com, are set up to point to my main domain. Because the Pixel is installed on a particular website, NOT a domain, I only need one Pixel (and Google Tracking ID) because each domain takes you to the same website. Facebook Pixels and Google Tracking IDs are installed on the website and are not associated with the domain.

That being said, there are some services that allow you to embed a Facebook Pixel or Google Tracking ID into a particular link. Linkfire and SmartURL do this. This only makes it so you can see the data of who is clicking on your links in Facebook Business Manager or Google Analytics rather than having to go to your Linkfire or SmartURL accounts. Keep mind, you pay for this convenience but it's not necessary.

For Google Analytics, you need to have a Google Account set up (Gmail, YouTube, etc.). Once you have that done, then you go to analytics.google.com to set up your Analytics account. Once there, you can create a new Google Tracking ID by clicking "Create Property" and entering in the web address you want to track. Similar to my Facebook Pixel, I only need to create one Tracking ID because all of my domains point to the same place.

Both Facebook Pixels and Google Tracking IDs track the same things. It's a good idea to have them both set up even if you only ever use Facebook's Business Manager over Google Analytics, for instance, because you never know when you'll need one or the other for something. Certain external services only allow Google Analytics codes, for instance. Also, when you create an ad on Google or on Facebook, the Google Tracking ID or Facebook Pixel play better together with the ad that was created on their respective platform. In short – just create both so it's done.

Personally, I use Facebook Business Manager more. I find it easier to navigate and understand. The layout makes more sense to me and the tools seem easier to find and use.

Facebook Ad Accounts and Google Adwords

You may want to run online ad campaigns to promote a show or a release. But did you ever think about running an online ad campaign to better understand the people interested in what you're doing? It works and, again, Facebook and Google have great tools to do it with.

I mentioned about that when you create you Facebook Business Manager profile, you probably want to go ahead and create an Ad Account that is linked to you Facebook Page as well. After creating your Google Analytics account, you probably want to also create your Google AdWords account, too. For beginners, I would recommend using AdWords Express as it's much simpler to use (even for someone who is more advanced with AdWords).

In either platform, when creating an add, you'll get to choose who the audience of that particular ad should be in terms of demographics, interests, key words, etc. You'll then be able to set a budget that is affordable for you and a duration of the ad campaign and the - BAM - you're done. Then, you'll able to see data on the people you click on your ad, which will better help you to understand the type of people you're attracting to your website, your music, your Facebook Page, your mailing list, etc.

Keep in mind that it's important to also understand how your ads will be run. For instance, when you run an ad on Facebook, you generally will use pictures or video mixed with a phrase and a call to action such as "Learn More" or "Chat in Messenger". That ad could then run on facebook.com, Messenger, Instagram's news feed, Instagram stories and other places. However, if you post an ad on Google, you will more than likely not have any photos or video and the ads will appear in Google search results or on other websites that have Google ads shown on them. Both options are good and will reach a very wide audience however in my experience a Google ad likely to be shown to more people as Facebook ads tend to only be shown to people who are using a Facebook-owned platform.

No matter which method you use, you will gain valuable data on your fans that will influence future ads, music, marketing, etc.

Short URLs and Link Tracking

A short URL allows you to take a long URL (a web address) and create a shortened link that appears more professional and is generally easier to type out because it has considerably less characters. Typically, these services also allow you to track and obtain certain analytic data on the people who use the link. You can even purchase your own shortened domain from any platform that sells domain names (such as GoDaddy). Most of the popular smart URL websites have a tie in with certain online marketing managers such as Zapier and Hubspot. I would highly recommended picking a service to track your links from and then any time you give out a link, give one of the trackable links out rather than the longer direct link. For instance, when I give out my Instagram account in an email newsletter, I wouldn't use www.insagram.com/mattannecharico but I would use http://bit.ly/mattinstag. This allows me to collect some very useful data about my fans.

My personal favourite is Bitly. For their free tier, you can have 10,000 links and 500 links under a branded short domain that you may own. But there are many others out there. Find what works for you. smartURL and Linkfire also have similar and, in many cases, more advanced capabilities to Bitly. They have limited features on their free tiers but what makes them special is that they were made specifically for the music industry. You can create special landing pages with links to your music on various websites, track analytics, etc. You will hear people in the industry talking about these two quite a lot but at an early stage in your career you probably don't need it. I might even say they are a bit overpriced considering all of the alternative free options out there.

The key take away from this section: whenever you are giving out a link, make it a trackable link so you can collect data. Whether it's a link to your music on Spotify or to your artist website, using a link-tracking service will tell you details about demographics and how people are interacting with you.

Built-in Data Tracking

Many of the website-building platforms such as Wix, Squarespace and WordPress will have their own built-in tracking tools. I would encourage you to ensure that these are enabled and frequently looked at because they could be important. Often, though, if you've installed Facebook Pixel and/or Google Tracking ID onto your website correctly (make sure to test it) then you will gain better results from these. But if you're on your Wix account because you're editing your website and you want to just quickly look at some stats, you might be able to get the basics from the built-in resources rather than opening another browser window to access the external data.

E-mail Marketing Managers

You need to have an e-mail marketing database. Don't try to get around it. Even if it means that, at first, you only have family and friends, then so be it. But get it set up because once you begin doing marketing for a single, an EP or album, or a performance, you want people to be able to easily sign up to stay in touch. Believe it or not, email marketing is still a vital part in how you need to communicate with your fans. It seems strange in our day and age of Social Media however it is still important and should not be forgotten. Later, it could also be used as a tool to obtain sponsorships from other companies but thats a conversation for another book.

ReverbNation provides a great free e-mail marketing platform called "Fan Reach" that allows fans to easily signup for your mailing list both on the platform or through an embeddable widget you can place on your website. You then can create great professional emails to everyone who signs up. Services like Wix and Squarespace also have fantastic email marketing managers that do very similar things. You may also opt to use a service like Mailchimp or ConstantContact, which are external platforms that specialise in email marketing. Find the best one for you at this point in your career by looking at each available option and then stick with it. Try not to have things all over the place because it will just make your life difficult. If you begin using something like MailChimp but later end up hosting your website at Wix and decide to use their email marketing manager instead then just make sure to export your mailing list from MailChimp (usually in a .cv format) and then import it into your new Wix database.

Whichever platform you choose, you will be able to get some data from these sources as well. First, you'll be able to see how many people are opening your emails as well as how many people have not. You will also have access to data like your click-through rate which tells you when people are clicking on links that you had included in a particular email. This data is important because it can tell you if your emails are interesting enough for your audience and if you're doing a good enough job at enticing your followers to view your external content. If, for instance, you created a link in a sentence at the end of a marketing email and people are clicking on it then it could tell you that people are actually reading your email entirely AND the information was interesting enough to want to click the link to learn more. If people are only clicking on links at the top of your email then it

59

could mean that your emails aren't interesting and people aren't reading it. It could also be telling you that the link at the bottom may not be as interesting to your audience as the link on the top. Either way, its good information to know! Then, if you've been smart and the links you've included in the email are from one of the trackable resources above then you'll be able to gain even more valuable information.

Messenger Bots

I think this is an important topic to cover at this point because in the two years Facebook has opened it up for Pages to install Messenger bots, this feature is beginning to change how people who run a Facebook Page communicate with its followers. Firstly, what is a Messenger Bot? Someone who creates a Messenger bot is creating a guided conversation that someone from the public can have within Facebook Messenger. Try out the Dreamscope Messenger bot (which is still being built but it is currently live) to get an idea for what it's like as a consumer. It's a way for the public to get information quicker and more organically but it is also a way for businesses to collect data from their customers.

In 2018, I was hired by a university to build the first ever Facebook Messenger bot for their employment service. The bot had to do several things: determine what the relationship was between the university and the person interacting with the bot (current student, former student, prospective student, staff member, other); and collect information about the students (former and current) such as their program of study, the year they graduate or graduated, and their student number for tracking purposes. All of this information was collected the very first time that someone interacted with the bot so that any information that a student requested from the bot in the future was relevant to their course of study. For instance, if they said to the bot "I need help with a CV" the bot would recognise the degree the student is or was on and would only give them CV advice relevant to their field. It also regularly recommended to the student that they meet with their careers advisor and provided the contact information of the advisor that was assigned to their department. All of this was automated. Then, if the employment centre had any announcements or opportunities that they wanted to push out to people who previously had interacted with the bot, they could choose to push it out to everyone or maybe only to graduates from a particular department for instance. Pretty cool, huh?

The statistics show that the open rates for an announcement made through Facebook Messenger is about 90 percent. This is staggering considering that the typical open rate for an email marketing campaign is between 10 percent and 20 percent. The few studies that have been done about Messenger bots show that people are almost 50 percent more likely to do business with a company who has a Facebook Messenger bot than those Pages who do not. As a result, it wouldn't be smart not to mention this as a great tool to think about using in conjunction with your email distribution list. Don't forget this could also be a way to collect email addresses if you program your bot to ask the user to provide it. A great platform for building Messenger bots is ManyChat but there are several others out there you can try. A word of advice, however, is that it can be complex and there are many rules Facebook has about how these bots can behave. Break these rules and you could risk being kicked off Facebook.

An alternative to a full-blown Messenger bot is to simply ask people to sign up to your Facebook Messenger broadcast list. People would simply send your Page a Facebook Message and your pre-programmed response thanking them for signing up for updates would reply and that would be the end of it. Then every time you want to send a broadcast (just like every time you want to send a marketing email campaign), you would log into the platform that you used to create the Messenger broadcast list and create a campaign to be sent out on Messenger. An artist who famously does this is Imogen Heap. She uses a great platform called Sendmate for this that's free up to 250 subscribers. The down side of using this method instead of a full-blown Messenger bot is that the data you collect is limited and you cannot collect a user's email address. Even if you used a full-on Messenger bot you risk the chance that Facebook one day could go under and suddenly all the data you collected is useless. Hard to see that happening but it's worth pointing out. Therefore, I would say that a Facebook Messenger bot (like one built using ManyChat) or something similar to a bot but not a full blown bot (such as Sendmate) is a great option for collecting data and interacting with your fans however use it in conjunction with your email campaigns and not instead of. I suspect we will be seeing more platforms like WhatsApp, for instance, that open up to bots in the future. Stay tuned.

Spotify and Apple Artist Accounts

Your aggregator or distributor will no doubt provide you with sales data. However, as is the case more often than not, this data is usually delayed several months. The folks at Spotify and Apple have made it possible for you to claim your Artist Account so that you can see data on streaming and downloading activity from their platforms automatically. Even more helpful is you can give access to these accounts to the rest of your artist team to help them better understand your demographics. The data learned from these sources can prove very valuable because you will learn things such as your most popular songs, age and gender demographics, the geographic area where your music is being accessed and more. Once you know this information, you may want to do some heavy marketing on Facebook or Google in a particular region, or maybe you want to travel there to perform. It is also helpful to know whether your music is accessed more via streaming or downloading as this will tell you a lot about your fans' psychographics. Other benefits include being able to add photographs, biography, tour and merch information, etc. Make sure to request access to your accounts. You will find it very helpful. Also, don't forget to download the apps for each to be able to monitor your stats on the go!

Apple: http://artists.apple.com
Spotify: http://artists.spotify.com

Artists

Artists

Collect Listener Feedback

One of the most powerful analytics data you can collect is direct feedback from listeners. I spent a lot of time collecting this feedback from people all over the world using a service called Jango. Jango is an internet radio station that allows artists to upload their tracks and pair them with similar tracks done by big name acts. Listeners then have the option to leave comments on the tracks. I collected hundreds of comments from listeners in every part of the world that I then used in my press kit. Unfortunately, it's not a free tool, but it's not very expensive either, and the returns you'll reap by pairing your songs right are more than worth the small investment. But keep in mind that you're likely to annoy listeners if your metal song gets played alongside a Carry Underwood song. If you want the most for your money then pair your song up with songs and/or artists that are very similar to you. This way, listeners are more likely to comment.

Check it out: www.radioairplay.com

Your Artist Website

YES, you need one. Don't try to avoid it. Facebook Pages, ReverbNation and SoundCloud don't cut it. In fact, if your dot com directed to one of these social media websites, then you might look very amateur. I spoke with a band recently who told me that other local bands only use Facebook for their artist website and those who choose to have websites didn't ever seem to update them. This was the reason that they didn't see a point in having one. My reply to them was simple: do you want to be a local band? If so – that's great but if you want to be anything more than a local band, and you want to be taken serious, then you need to have an artist website that is regularly maintained. It's just a part of the gig!

Your artist website is the central hub of your artist business and all of the other platforms are simply extensions of it. There is no reason why you shouldn't have an artist website especially now that so many out of the box platforms like Bandzoogle, Squarespace, and Wix exist. If that hasn't convinced you as to why you need to have an artist website then how about the fact that creating your own site is absolutely essential to the success of your online marketing efforts for one reason: control. You don't the same control on Facebook or ReverbNation.

The very foundation of this book and in fact of Dreamscope is to truly give control to independent artists. As cliché as it is, the phrase "knowledge is power" exists because it's true. The very fact that you are able to record and release music on your own now is a prime example of the shift in control from label to artists. While social media sites are important for a number of reasons, they do take away your control in a lot of ways. So when building your website, let's look at some key things you'll want to consider.

The User Experience

The design and usability of your website is incredibly important. Of course you should do whatever necessary to make an awesome website but if people can't easily find what they need or interact with you once they get there then you're wasting your time. Make sure the website is easy to maneuver and that information can be easily absorbed. Everything down to the navigation and feel of the website should be considered before it gets published. Here are some quick pointers:

Don't hide your menu. Sure, it might look clean to have it all collapsed into a little button in the corner that people can click on to see when they want it, but sometimes it can be confusing. Instead, use the navigation bar as a way for people to quickly understand what the purpose of your site is simply by seeing it!

Use the band or artist logo at the top and make sure the fonts used on the website are consistent with those used on the album artwork. This creates a sense of cohesion and affirms to the public that this is in fact an official website for this artist or band.

Allow people to quickly access your social media channels and sign up for your mailing list. This can easily be done by having little buttons in the header of the website so that it will continue to appear on every page someone visits.

By providing people with the opportunity to stream high quality versions of your tracks from your website, you are ensuring that they will be more likely to sign up for your mailing list and become a fan. Remember MySpace? That's why it worked so well for artists. Wherever your music is posted on the site, make sure there are external links posted so your fans know what platforms your music can be streamed on. It also makes it easier for them to follow you on those platforms. Odds are, when they are in their car, they won't go to your website on their mobile device to stream your music. They will open up a streaming platform.

Avoid being text heavy. People skim read. At most, you get 15 to 20 seconds to impress people enough to make them want to stay on your website. Use it wisely! Instead of text, give them video, images, and music.

Make sure your images and graphics don't take long to load. You can keep the file sizes small and still retain quality. Also, don't overuse flash. People will get bored waiting for these things to load and just leave. Plus, remember that most people are looking at your website on a mobile device.

Make sure that your website looks good on a phone and tablet. Duh!

Content and context are also important factors to consider when looking at the user experience and they work hand in hand. You can spend loads of time creating great content but if it's presented in a way that makes absolutely no sense to the viewer then the message will be lost. Content that you'll want to consider having on your website in order to help tell your story includes:

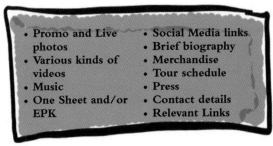

- Promo and Live photos
- Various kinds of videos
- Music
- One Sheet and/or EPK
- Social Media links
- Brief biography
- Merchandise
- Tour schedule
- Press
- Contact details
- Relevant Links

Photos

Some areas are okay for cutting corners, and you should. Any business would. Never cut corners with promotional photos. Fantastic promotional photos help you look more professional and can be used for a very long time. They're simply a great investment. Trust me on this one - spend the money here. When you're doing promotional photos for an album, it's important that the photos have the same feel as the music. If you're doing a rap album and you take photographs of yourself somewhere in the fields wearing jeans and a button-up shirt with a fedora on then you're going to be in some serious trouble.

It's important that you do some homework pertaining to the photographer as well. Look at their previous work and take note of things such as how the photographer has the subject posed, the lighting, the kind of editing the photographer uses, the locations they shoot in particularly if they shoot inside or outside, and their overall style. Much like an audio engineer, photographers have a set of go-to tools that they use when working and therefore their final product has a style to it that is unique to the photographer. It's very important to pay attention to details like this because then you'll have a better idea of what your final product will likely be.

Biographies

Writing a biography can be a very awkward experience, but it really doesn't have to be. While it feels weird talking about yourself, remember that you should be the one to tell your own story and this is your chance! I would recommend that you go and read the biographies of other artist to get an idea of the tone and how it's written. Even though fans might read your biography, it isn't intended for them. It is intended for the media and people in the industry. One of the hardest things is remembering that people who visit your website have a very short attention span; they want short, sweet, and to the point. If it's too long people will take one look at it and move on. If there's too much "fluff" and your biography doesn't get to the point quickly enough, people will be less likely to read it. By "fluff" I mean things like anything that sounds emotional or anything that pads the biography such as unnecessary words. Of course, there are artists biographies that are longer. The only time it should be longer is if you've got more that people need to know. Think along the lines of career highlights, impressive venues you've played at, album sales/streams, awards, impressive collaborations, etc. If an artists' biography is longer for any reason other than that then it's likely "fluff" and people simply won't read it.

As a general rule of thumb, I recommend no more than 4 paragraphs in this order:

1. A brief intro about who you are, what you do, and any related professional associations you have;
2. A brief bit about your influences, an interesting quote from you, details on your style of music including big acts that your style may be similar to;
3. Notable releases, performances, collaborations, sales data, etc.;
4. What you're currently working on including projects in the near future.

Anything more than this and it's simply too much. And for goodness sake do not tell a chronological story. "Mark started singing when he was three years old because he was influenced by his parent's love for music. By the age of eight his parents bought him his first guitar. When he turned twelve his first band…" is such a boring biography. If you don't have a lot of experience, your biography is the perfect place to talk about your WHY. See? It's already becoming useful.

A final word on biographies: keep them updated regularly and consistent across all of your social media platforms, websites, and the like. Odds are the above platforms will contain a longer biography. That being said, you should also have a prepared biography that's no more than 500 words, a common request from some media outlets.

Effective Use of Media

You are a content creator even if all you're doing to recording music. It's important for the user's experience that they be able to have access to the media you're creating. Here are some general best practices:

Offer Full Tracks. Giving only 30-second previews of your tracks on your artist website is another thing the industry did as a result of being scared by the piracy debacle in the early 2000s. The idea was to entice listeners to have to purchase the song in order to hear it in its entirety but thanks to streaming this is an outdated way of thinking. And really - why wouldn't you want to give them the full track to listen to? Think about it: most people listen to music on the go now. If they wanted to listen to your music on the go, they aren't going to go to your website to stream it for free. They will go to streaming platforms where you'll at least get a small fee for that free stream. But when fans are searching for you online and want to listen to your music, let them listen to it right then and there! There's actually research that shows if you allow the listener to experience the full song, they're more likely to buy it later.

Video. This is important. Your website must have video. I'm not just talking about a music video. There are so many different kinds of video content that can and often should appear on your artist website. A video diary, live streaming while you're in the studio or rehearsing, from a gig that you're doing, announcing events, talking about your songs, behind the scenes on tour, and so on. Websites like Mogulus, Stickam, and uSream offer ad-supported webcast capability with a fairly easy set up. The cloud-hosting platform Six has even started offering the capability to live stream. Statistics from Forbes.com show that internet video traffic will account for more than 80 percent of all consumer internet traffic in the next few years and that live streaming will account for 13 percent of all of that. Furthermore, they have found that 64 percent of consumers purchase after watching videos. Do I need to give you any more reason?

EPKs and One Sheets

EPK stands for "electronic press kit," and it's the digital form of the press kits people used to send out in the mail as recently as the early 2000s. Usually it was a nice branded pocket folder, either with the logo of the artist/band or of their representative, and inside would be at least one promotional photograph, news clippings, a biography, contact details, upcoming shows, details on recognition, and sometimes a stage plot. Now, all of this can more simply be combined in a simple PDF however there are some in the industry that ask for physical press kits. If you've got an EPK, make sure that it can easily be printed on nice thick paper and that the designs work well in print just as they do in PDF. Alternatively, you can have one for print and one for PDF but to me this is too complicated. Keep it simple.

When you send out your EPK, if you're going to attach it in an email, make sure that the file size is small. Nothing annoys people more than having a large attachment filling up their email inbox or having to download a large PDF on a mobile device. Make it as easy as possible for them to access the information you want them to see. I've seen artists create an EPK as a private page on their website and then they simply send this link to people. I've seen people who create a landing page for people in the industry that simply asks them to fill in details about who they are in order to gain access to the EPK. There are several companies out there that allow you to create EPKs on their platform and then simply use the link to the EPK instead of attaching a file in an email. SonicBids, ReverbNation, and Bandzoogle are some of the most popular. They have free versions, but to gain access to the features you'll probably want, you're going to have to pay. Personally, I would design my own. In fact I did. I used SonicBids for a period of time and they were great when they first started. I booked a lot of gigs through them. However much like many businesses in the music industry who start out promising to help independent musicians, they lost their way. One year I even saw an advertisement that they had placed in the program that was passed out to everyone attending the Grammy's. Because,

Just Thought You Should Know

you know, people nominated for Grammy's are in their target market. You can't see it, but I'm rolling my eyes right now.

If you don't have enough to fill out an electronic press kit, then I would recommend at least creating a One Sheet. One Sheets are typically done to promote a particular project and contains most of what would be in a press kit except it's on one page. Your artist or band name, contact details, biography, a photo or several photos and details about an upcoming release is all information that should be included on the one sheet. The practicality of a one sheet is that it's a more simplified version of a press kit that's easier and quicker for the reader. In fact, some artists have a press kit as well as a one sheet that's used to help promote a particular project.

No matter how you decide to go about doing it, it's always a great idea to have your EPK or one sheet available to download from your website or, if you use an external platform, have a link to it created and placed in a location or in location that make sense.

Online Presence and Search Engine Optimisation

When you want to get information about something, where do you go? I doubt your answer was your local library. The internet is responsible for the simple dissemination of information to any part of the world instantly, and you need to be there. When people type your artist or band name into an internet search engine, you should be at the top or at least close to it and if you're not then people are simply not going to be able to easily find you. Not addressing this early on is so silly because it's actually a very easy fix. This is referred to as Search Engine Optimisation (SEO).

First, any platform that allows you to create a free artist profile, do it! Make sure it contains links to your website and social media, your updated pictures, and an updated biography. Popular ones are ReverbNation, OurStage, Bandzoogle, Bandcamp, as well as lyric websites such as Metrolyrics.com and letssingit.com. This is in addition to the usual social media websites like Facebook, Twitter, Instagram, Soundcloud, YouTube and yes even LinkedIn.

It's not enough to have these profiles set up and filled with content and links back to your artist website. You need to link them to one another too. Having a successful linking strategy is essential because the internet is full of search engine "crawlers" that look through websites and find commonality. They sort of help to bring order to the chaos by identifying that, when you type in a particular term, it's related to all of these different websites. If you've got everything pointing to your website and to your social media channels, then the internet's crawlers will recognise that they are related and group them all together so that when someone types in your artist or band name they appear together and at the top.

Next, make sure that when you use photos or videos on your website or anywhere on the web that you edit the details to contain your name. That way, when search engine crawlers are looking through websites, they will notice that the photograph is related to you make it more likely to appear when someone types in your name. Similarly, on YouTube or Facebook videos, it's important to put your name as a tag in the metadata for this same reason. Basically, any digital content where you're able to add tags, make sure your name is one of them.

Marketing Platforms

When I started my career I wish just one of the many marketing platforms currently out there to help you with your online marketing were available. Before releasing a project you should spend some time exploring your options. Sign up for the free accounts and see what they have to offer. Maybe you'll find one that you want to use, maybe you'll realise that there are way to do the same things on your own and therefore you don't need to use them, or maybe you'll find inspiration for something else. The important thing is that you play around with the tools available to you. One of my favourites is ToneDen. A good friend of mine uses another awesome platform called Found.ee. There are many others out there so take a look around and have some fun coming up with new ways to engage with your fans. This should be exciting! Remember that marketing is essentially the

Just Thought You Should Know

way you get to creatively tell your story and platforms like ToneDen are designed to help make this easier and automated.

What Is Your Market

Thanks to technology, we've seen power and opportunity shift from those who have long been gatekeepers in the music industry to the so-called bedroom musicians who can write, record and instantly release music to digital stores around the world. Technology has made it simple, and as a result of this shift there are increasingly more people releasing music than ever before. This makes it harder for an artist to differentiate themselves. But there are some relatively simple ways to stand out that I think are really important for you to know.

The 80:20 Rule

It's important for you to understand that your goal as an artist shouldn't be to try and get everyone around the world to love your music. It ain't gonna happen, my friend, and you'd totally wear yourself out trying. Instead, I want you to focus on this awesome theory called the 80:20 rule. This is an economic concept that states that 80 percent of your business is only going to come from 20 percent of the listeners. Therefore, you should be focusing on maximising the relationship you are created with the 20 percent instead of focusing on the entire population. But who are your 20 percent? That's where the idea of niche marketing comes in.

Niche Marketing

Because traditional models of marketing to the public aren't as effective as they once were, niche marketing has become the answer. This allows you to make music for your fans rather than finding fans for your music. By understanding your WHY, you will be able to identify what makes you relatable as a human being and thus you will be able to find your "tribe". Thing of stereotypes. They exist for a reason. Rockers will likely dress, act, walk, talk, do, and think very differently from a hipster. One might be more conservative and one might be a bit more liberal. One might like to read things digitally while the other might prefer to have a print out. Yes, these are labels and as a musician it can be annoying to put a label on yourself let alone other people but these have been used in the marketing world for many years for a reason: they work. So embrace it for this moment. These are "your people".

Demographics and Psychographics

Demographics have long been used by marketers to target someone's current or potential fan base. Demographics include things like gender, income, education, occupation, age, sexual orientation, and so on. This was often the way that marketers would decide which country and then which part of that country to place certain ads, what kind of imagery to use, what radio stations to target, what magazines to be in, and more. It's very important to have an understanding of your demographics. Your sales reports from your distributor will often tell you their geographic location but now, thanks to services like Spotify and Apple opening up portals for artists, you're able to see a great deal more of the demographic information of the people listening to your music. But you should be doing more. Notice where other artists are playing who have a similar style as you and try to play in the same venues. Then, while you're on stage, try to take note of the people in the audience. If you notice that there are quite a number of 50 year olds jamming to your music despite the fact that you've thought all along that 20 somethings would be your market then you should definitely be rethinking your strategy. Finally, do some research on the people who are fans of bands that are similar to yours. Thanks to Facebook pages, this is more easily done today than ever before. It wouldn't be a stretch to think that a band that sounds like yours would attract a similar audience.

Psychographics, in my opinion, are more important for you to understand in today's world. They are traits relatable to a more specific segment of the population. Demographics provide a more factual look at a person whereas psychographics look at shared interests regardless of demographics. If you are able to identify enough shared traits that you have with others then you'll be able to identify a more effective niche market for yourself. Instead of having an outward facing view of the world, psychographics require you to first have an inward facing one. Hence, the push to understand your WHY as clearly as possible. Identify your own interests and strengths as a person and then find groups of people that share them. Does your likely fan live on a mobile device all day, or do they like to live outside of electronics as much as possible? Do they read? If so, what do they read? How do they read - online or in print? What do they like to do in their spare time? Do they enjoy going to clubs or do they prefer to go for walks in the park? This is also a much more creative way to identifying a market for yourself than simply using demographics.

A great example that I read about once was a band called the Decemberists. The band was known for things such as their their lyrics, a love for 1960s British folk, their support of Barack Obama in the 2008 presidential campaign, and a dispute they had with Stephen Colbert. If you took a moment to think about these traits they might tell you that the band's target audience is likely pretty literate, left-leaning consumers with a great music collection. You could then take it a step further and identify artists that also fall into these individual categories and BOOM - you have a target market. If you think your target market is likely to be coffee drinkers then you need to slap your lyrics on a coffee mug - SOLD! Give this some serious thought. Having gone through your WHY as thoroughly as possible will guide this process.

The key is to identify who you are as a person, what makes you stand out, what makes you relatable and who are the people you would likely relate to, and what those people who relate to you will likely want from you.

Let's Talk Music Publishing

Oh boy, this is a fun one but I really think that you should know at least the basics about it. Music publishing is unnecessarily complicated so much so that people who work in music publishing even get confused sometimes. Generally speaking, there are two kinds of publishing contracts. First, the most common kind of publishing agreement is the individual song agreement or the exclusive agreement. For a single composition agreement, the songwriter will transfer the copyrights of a select number of compositions to a publisher and as a result the publisher pays the songwriter a portion of the income derived from the exploitation of that copyright. With an exclusive agreement, the songwriter agrees to transfer the copyright of all compositions created for a specified period of time in exchange for a portion of the income earned from their exploitation.

Second, is the publishing administration deal. Under this agreement, the songwriter assigns the publisher the right to administer certain compositions for a specified period of time while the songwriter retains the full copyright of the composition. Under this kind of deal, the publisher chargers a fee of 10 to 25 percent of any publishing income made. Administering rights to a song means that the publisher essentially does all of the work of registering a composition with worldwide PROs and collects licensing fees, among other administration-type tasks.

What A Music Publisher Does

As vague as the phrase may be, a music publisher is so important that they represent half of the income that a musical composition can generate. That's a big deal! They play an integral part in many processes within the music industry and I would argue are often unsung heroes. Below is a list of the main responsibilities of a music publisher to help put it into perspective:

- Register musical compositions with performing rights organisations worldwide;
- Secures placements for a song in film, television, video games, advertisements, and so on;
- Arranges for the manufacturing and distribution of sheet music and other music-related books;
- Takes action against those who infringe on the copyright of a musical composition and negotiates settlement fees;
- Supports emerging songwriters through songwriting development and songwriting camps;
- Finances and facilitates the recording of demos;

- Pitches compositions to labels, artists, or an artist's representative to secure commercially released recordings
- Issues appropriate mechanical licenses and negotiates fees

Music Licensing

When a copyright owner sells permission to − or "licenses" − a third party to utilise its copyright controls, a deal needs to be done between the copyright owner and the licensee. This is what happens in a publishing contract you might sign as a songwriter but it also happens in a recording contract that you might sign as a recording artist. In the music industry, there are three main ways copyright owners license copyright controls. Which method is used generally depends on what the licensee wants to do with the song or the recording.

Option One: Direct License

This is when the licensee finds the copyright owner and negotiates a bespoke deal. This happens when a brand, for instance, wants to use your song or recording in an advertisement. They must find you or your publisher, if you have one, and make an offer. You or your publisher will negotiate a deal, agree to the terms, and then write a contract (DON'T forget the contract).

Option Two: License via a third party

This way of licensing happens when the copyright owner allows a third party to license on his or her behalf. The third party then does the deal on behalf of the copyright owner. Streaming platforms like Apple Music and Spotify cannot possibly negotiate a deal with every DIY artist so they have instead done deals with aggregators like TuneCore, CDBaby and Distrokid. When you distribute to streaming services using an aggregator or a traditional distributor that has a deal with Spotify, for instance, you are allowing them to negotiate these licenses on your behalf.

Option Three: License via the collective licensing system

In some cases, the music industry comes together and licenses as one big happy family. The idea being that negotiation power is greater when we come together to negotiate than if we were to negotiate alone. A perfect example of this is with the company Merlin, who represents the digital rights of more than 800 record labels all over the world. There are also collective licensing societies for songwriters and music publishers too. Licensees can then get two "blanket licenses", one covering all recordings form DIY artists or record labels and one covering all compositions. The collecting societies collect the money and pass it on to the artists, labels, writers and publishers, in theory based on how often their music was used.

Collecting Societies

Collecting societies are companies that fall under the category of a Performing Rights Organisation, or PRO as it's commonly referred to. There are two categories of collecting societies – societies that collect for the songwriters and publishers for performing rights as well as societies that collect for recording copyright owners for mechanical rights. An example of collection societies that collect the performing rights for a composition is ASCAP and BMI in the United States and PRS for Music in the United Kingdom. Examples of collection societies that collect mechanical royalties are SoundExchange in the United States and PPL in the United Kingdom. As a songwriter you should join one of the societies that collect for songwriters but if you release your own music you should also make sure to join the societies that collect mechanical royalties.

Let's Talk Music Tech

If you don't know a thing about music technology, such as DAWs (Digital Audio Workstations like ProTools or Logic), plugins, and the crazy amount of outboard gear that any given studio might use, that's okay. I don't believe you have to. But I do believe that, in order to be able to talk the talk when you're recording in a studio or performing live at a gig, you should understand some fundamentals. It just makes you look more professional and will also help you to give a better performance. What fundamentals are need-to-know is a debatable topic, but I'm going to give you list based on what has helped me as an artist.

I cannot stress this enough: I'm going to cover only the very basics here in order to make it so you can communicate with a sound person about certain things that can impact your performance. I would recommend checking out any one of the amazing books out there about setting up a home studio to familiarise yourself with more of this. Again, if you're not interested in sound tech, then don't try to become a pro. Still, make sure you know some of the basics. The more you know, the less someone else will have to make decisions for you.

Digital Audio Workstations (DAWs)

There are so many DAWs on the market and while they each have similarities, they are each very different and sometimes used for different reasons. In fact, explaining them is so complex that you will generally only find that a single book is used to explain a single DAW. You should have a general understanding of how to run at least one of them whether it's for recording demos on your own or even just to be able to talk with a sound engineer in a language he or she understands. GarageBand is a free DAW offered for Apple computers and is a great stepping stone to learning Logic Pro. Another great free option is Audacity, which runs on both PC, Apple, and Linux computers. ProTools is arguably the most advanced of the DAWs on the market and is much more complicated to learn but also much more widely used in the high end recording studios and broadcast centres. Depending on things such as the genre of music you make, certain DAWs offer better native plugins than other do. Plugins are what we call the digital versions of all of the physical pieces of equipment that recording studios typically have (called out-board gear) such dynamic processors, time-based processors, and more. A 'native plugin' is a plugin that comes with the DAW and not one from an external company like WAVES. Remember that as an artist you shouldn't be concerned with becoming 100 percent proficient in everything but have a basic understanding of how things work. You should know how to add new tracks to a session in your chosen DAW and how to record, erase, cut and add effects to the tracks. Play around with a DAW. You'll thank me later.

Your HOW includes the people on your artist team but it also includes the tools that you use to realise your WHY. As this is where the majority of the work actually gets done, this has been a very long section, but we've made it! I could've written a much more comprehensive version of this chapter, but it would've taken up volumes. Still, I hope that the things we've covered here kick-start those creative juices in your brain enough to go and explore topics I haven't covered. I've learned over the years that being a jack of all trades but a master of none is one of the best ways to live. You're not going to know everything about everything and that's one reason why we collaborate with others. Sure, you'll have things that you specialise in because you know more about them and have a greater interest in them. But to be a jack of all trades is the only way to ensure that you have an idea of what is happening in every stage of the process in order to avoid being screwed over. It doesn't mean being an expert at everything. It also doesn't mean doing everything on your own. It simply means you're able to be in control of your own career the way I believe you should be.

Signal Flow

The easiest way to think about signal flow: it's the journey a sound takes to get to the listener's ears, beginning with the source of the sound. A vocalist, for instance, produces sound with his or her vocal chords. This sound then travels through the air and is captured by some kind of transducer, usually a microphone in this case. Then the sound is converted into an electric signal that's sent through many other electronics that do different things to the signal: pre-amplifiers, recording or live-sound desks, effects processors, amplifiers, speakers, etc. Then the signal is finally converted back into something that can be heard by the human ear. The easiest way to think of signal flow is as a diagram. I have made up a common signal flow chart for you, which can be found at the end of this chapter.

Compression and Limiting

These are two of the most commonly used tools, especially in a recording studio. But many live audio technicians use them as well. As a musician, particularly a vocalist, it's important to understand what these are because they can affect how you perform at any given moment of a song. When you're in the studio, if you understand what compression does to your voice, you'll be able to notice once it's been applied and to communicate with the engineer about it.

Compression smoothly reduces audio's dynamic range. Dynamic range is the difference between the soft parts and the loud parts of a piece of audio. As a vocalist, compression is helpful because there may be parts of a song that you sing incredibly soft but then later in the song you might do some loud belting. The difference between the soft parts and the loud, belting parts (the dynamic range) are reduced, making the loud parts softer so that the overall level can be increased. Of course having good mic technique helps here as well, but that's a discussion for another book. Compression can be used on everything from vocals to different parts of a song, including percussion, guitars, piano, and more. After applying compression to the individual instrument, audio engineers will often then add compression to the overall mix of a song. All modern music uses compression to some degree. To get a better idea of what compression does, plug your instrument or a microphone into your audio interface and use the free compressors that come with you DAW. Play around with the compression by changing the settings and listening to what it does to your sound.

Limiting often works together with compression. In fact, it can be considered an extreme form of compression. Limiting is basically a tool that totally prevents the sound from going above a certain volume. If the sound goes beyond these points then it is adjusted according to the limits that you've set. In general, limiting is used to prevent a sound from "clipping".

Time-based Effects

Time-based effects are used to add depth to a particular sound or even to the overall mix. They are referred to as time-based effects because they alter the time and usually the manner in which a sound is heard. The two most used time-based effects are delay and reverb. While the two often get mixed up, the differences between them are pretty significant. Knowing the differences these will make to your sound can even alter the performance you give. Not to mention if you are trying to "fake it" with a sound guy and you get these two very basic things mixed up then your entire cover is blown. Better to know the difference.

Adding delay to a sound is basically saying to your DAW, "I want to hear this again in 15 milliseconds". Quite simply it's the repeating of the sound. The more technical explanation of delay is that it is when audio is stored directly into your computer's RAM and then after a specified length of time is read out again. Expertise usage of delay can get you an effect called "chorusing" and the perception of an echo. Reverb, on the other hand, is what gives the perception of the size, density, and nature of a space that a sound is heard in. Think of what it sounds like when a singer is performer in a massive arena as opposed to what it sounds like when they sing in their car. When you project sound, that sound will bounce off of the wall in front of you then onto the wall behind you and will continue bounce around the room unless something gets in its way. It can be a tricky thing but this is why studios put the blocks of foam on their wall for sound reinforcement so that the natural reverberation of the room is more controlled.

When I am in the studio recording, I go into it knowing that a ballad, for instance, is likely to have more time-based processors, such as reverb on my vocal, when the track is all mixed. Therefore, I prefer to have some in my headphones when I'm recording live because I will give a performance that takes it into account. Sometimes, this isn't possible, and you simply have to imagine it's there and perform accordingly.

Microphones

Microphones are a form of transducer that converts sound into electricity. There are three types of microphones: dynamic, ribbon, and condenser. Each are used in very different ways and their individual characteristics allow you to capture the performance of a particular instrument very differently.

Dynamic microphones work using the theory of electromagnetic induction, meaning that in order to convert sound into electricity the microphone contains a coil situated between two magnets that generates current. The most common dynamic microphone is the Shure SM58, which is generally more rugged and its usage and quite versatile, so it can be used on virtually any instrument without being damaged.

Ribbon microphones are similar to dynamics. They also use the theory of electromagnetic induction; however, in a ribbon microphone, a very thin and delicate piece of aluminium is situated in between the two magnets instead of a coil like in a dynamic microphone. You'll need to be careful not to ruin these delicate mics. Since this piece of ribbon is so small, its output signal is also very low, which means the ribbon microphone requires a transformer to be connected to it to boost the signal. Many of the vintage microphones used by the likes of Frank Sinatra or old radio broadcasts were ribbon microphones.

The condenser microphone is very different. It runs using the electrostatic principal. Two plates sit in its diaphragm, one in front and one in back. A resistor connects both of them and creates electrical charge. These microphones require something called phantom power to work. Phantom power is sent either from the recording desk or from the microphone preamp through pins two and three of an XLR, or mic, cable and into the microphone to power it. Sometimes, you may even need to wait a few minutes for the microphone to be properly powered up. The most famous kind of condenser microphone is the German-made Neumann microphone that was first made at the behest of Adolf Hitler to ensure he could be heard more clearly and loudly. Today, they remain one of the most sought after microphones in the world.

Most vocalist will use some kind of a dynamic microphone when performing live but will use a condenser microphone in the studio, although handheld wireless condenser microphones for stage performances do exist. While okay to use on a voice, you would not, however, want to us a ribbon microphone on a loud instrument like snare drum because you'd likely damage the ribbon. It's important to understand the kinds of microphones available and, even more important, what they are best used for.

The topics of microphones can get very in depth. For the sake of not overwhelming you with information, I've only provided you with the basic detail. I would suggest reading up on our good friend, the microphone, to learn more about its various uses, microphone placement, and more. It's good information to know. If you remember what I've just told you, then you're already going to sound like a pro.

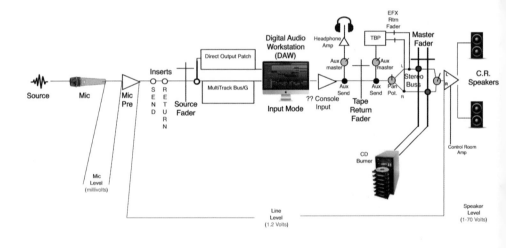

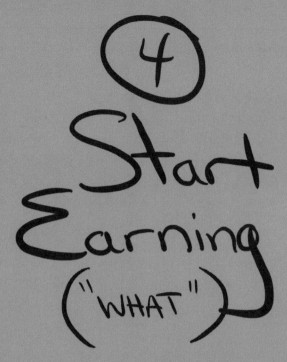

Your Results

You've come a long way, and you should be very proud of yourself! We have now reached the point where we get to your WHAT. Your WHY is an intangible thing like your beliefs, your morals, and what you stand for as an artist. Your WHAT is the tangible and measurable representation of your WHY. In many ways your WHAT is the result of your WHY. It's the point where you see the realisation of your own definition of success. As an artist, your WHAT could be finishing an album, gaining fans, or selling your music or merchandise. In some cases, your WHAT can also include earning awards for your work as well. It's important that you define WHAT you want your result to be in the most realistic way possible early on so that you can know the steps you need to make in order to achieve your desired outcome. Do yourself a favour with this: don't discount the baby steps. For instance, finishing the writing, recording, production, and distribution of an album is one hell of a WHAT and one that you should celebrate. But there's still work to be done after, so don't get lazy on me now.

Music Rights and Copyrights Explained

By now you've likely completed some kind of body of work, whether it's a recording or a collection of compositions. As a creator, you have a certain number of rights that are automatic and that allow you to turn your art into a money generating business. Without these rights, there would be no music business. The basis of absolutely everything you do in your artist business is based solely on the exploitation of your rights. To start, there are three main ways that you can make money from your work:

- Create and exploit your intellectual property (commonly referred to as IP)
- Stage and monetise live performances
- Build a fan base and monetise the fan relationship.

Lets dig in a bit more on these.

Intellectual Property

The entire music industry and indeed the entertainment industries as a whole are based around the exploitation of intellectual property, often referred to as IP. Most artists create four distinct kinds of IP. First, every song you write is protected by copyright. In the music industry we call these the "song rights" or the "publishing rights". Second, every recording you make is protected by a separate copyright. We call these the "recording rights" or the "master rights". You have to understand that in the recording industry, there is a copyright of the written composition, usually owned by the songwriter and/or the publishing company, and a totally separate copyright of any individual recording of the composition, usually owned by a record label or you, assuming you self-release your recordings. Third, all the photos and illustrations you create are also protected by copyright – the "artistic rights". Fourth, your brand – so your actual name, performer name or band name – can be protected by a thing called trademark. Trademarks have to be registered, which costs money, so they are not generally a top priority for new artists. However, copyright exists as soon as songs are written, recordings made, and visuals created, so you need to know a little bit about copyright from the off.

Copyright Ownership

In most parts of the world copyrights are automatic once they take on a tangible form such as a piece of hand written work, a demo recording, a word processing document, and so on. This means that nobody formally claims ownership of the copyright in any one composition, recording, or visual piece of work so the law has to tell us who the default owners are. Thanks to The Berne Convention, which has been ratified by 177 of the 195 countries around the world, most countries agree that by default a creative copyright is owned by whoever created the work. By default a recording copyright is owned by whoever arranges for the recording to take place. By default the copyright in a photo or illustration is owned by the photographer or illustrator.

Where multiple people create a copyright-protected work together, they co-own the resulting copyright. This happens a lot with songwriting. If you co-write a composition with another person, you together co-own the composition copyright. It's for you as collaborators to decide how you are going to split the copyright and decide what percentage of the copyright (and any subsequent money) each individual gets. I would recommend many of the great programmes popping up to help automate this process. My personal favourite is auddly.com.

Copyright Assignment

It's important to note that, although copyright law provides these default ownership rules, copyrights can also be transferred. For example, one member of a band might arrange for a recording to take place and therefore be the default. He or she is the copyright owner. However, if they have a band agreement in place they might have decided to share the copyright with their bandmates. This is a perfect example of why having a band partnership agreement in place at the very beginning is so crucial. Another example is when it comes to a publishing contract or a recording contract in which you assign certain copyrights to the publisher or record label in order for them to carry out the exploitation of the work. Copyright law allows such transfer and calls it 'assignment'. Remember that there should always be a written agreement so everyone is clear on who owns what and for what period of time.

Term of Copyright

A copyright doesn't last forever even though it generally lasts for quite a long time. At the time of writing this book, the copyright for a musical composition, photograph or illustration in Europe and the United States lasts for the lifetime of the creator plus another 70 years. The copyright of a recording lasts 70 years from the first date of release in both the United States and in Europe.

Copyright Controls

Having a copyright means you have a set of automatic controls in what happens to that piece of work. In general, copyright gives you a set of six controls.

- The reproduction control
- The distribution control
- The rental control
- The adaptation control
- The performance control
- The communication control

In the music industry, the reproduction and distribution controls are often grouped together and referred to as the "reproduction rights" or "mechanical rights". The performance and communication controls are often grouped together and referred to as the "performing rights" or "neighbouring rights".

Just Thought You Should Know

Making Money from Music

Copyright makes money whenever a person or company wants to exploit one of your copyright controls. This means that someone wants to reproduce, or distribute, or rent, or adapt, or perform, or communicate one of your songs or your recordings. Whenever that happens, they must get your permission to exploit your copyright controls. Licensing is when you charge for your permission, which is how copyright makes money. Alternatively, you transfer the assignment of your copyright to another person or organisation, even if only for a certain period of time, who exploits those controls and you take a percentage the earnings.

> If you are gigging and performing your own songs in public, you can usually submit your set list to the PRO you are affiliated with as a songwriter and make money from the performances of those songs. Usually you have to have a promoter, venue owner or sound engineer sign off on your set lists but do not forget to submit your set lists to your PRO or you'll potentially be missing out on some money.

In the end, you should always take responsibility for the money you are or are not making from the content you create. "The buck stops with me" is a phrase often used by leaders of organisations because they understand that the direction of their team and thus the realisation of their or their company's WHY is completely up to them to see to fruition. If something is not working then you need to analyse why and then try something new. Maybe your message is confusing. Maybe your website layout is difficult to manoeuvre. Usually, it's the smallest changes that you need to make which ends up making the biggest difference in your earnings. It's easy to blame your team but it's not always easy to look at what you could've done differently. If your team didn't do what you wanted them to do then that means that you either picked the wrong team or you didn't provide them with adequate direction. If there was a problem with your team you probably would've recognised it at some point and if you decided not to address it then you don't get to complain when your WHAT isn't as good as you had planned. Own your success but own your failures and learn from them. This is part of the process.

Just Thought You Should Know

TYPE OF ROYALTY

Synchronisation ———
Mechanicals ———
Performance ———

Broadcasters

Clubs, Hotels, etc.

100% of Performance Licensing $$

PRS/ASCAP/GEMA
Performing Rights Organisation (PRO)

50% of NET Performance Royalty

Publisher

93.25% of Mechanical $$

Publisher's Agent

100% of Mechanical $$

Record Companies

100% of Synchronisation $$

Film Producers

Video Producers

50% of NET Performance Royalty

50% of Synchronisation $$

50% of Mechanical $$

Songwriter

Composition Royalty Flow Chart

Direct to Fan Marketing

I decided to put this bit in the WHAT section and not in the HOW section with the other bits about marketing for one main reason: this is a plan that you make long before, say, an album a release, but you carry it out immediately before and largely after the release. It's a plan that helps you put some structure to how you will interact with your fans and how you will monetise the relationships you're building with them. Remember that one of the three ways that you make money from your creative work is by monetising your relationship with your fans. There are many ways you can do this but not one prescription will work for everyone simply because YOU are different than everyone else. Your direct to fan marketing plan is just that - direct from YOU to your fans. It cannot come from your manager. It cannot come from your record label. It has to come from you to be authentic. Other parties may be able to help and guide you, but if it's not ultimately from you then your fans simply won't buy into it as much.

To begin, it's important you take a good, honest look at where you are at this very moment in terms of your following and your career. Key word: *honest*. For instance, you'll want to assess how many social media followers you have. Have you had any accomplishments in your career thus far, which can include anything from maybe your first gig or getting to study at a particular university or maybe recording your first single? Be honest, and don't sugarcoat anything. Maybe you're just getting started and don't have any followers - that's totally okay! Everyone starts there. But don't ever be afraid of being honest with yourself about it.

Then set some tangible and measurable goals for yourself. Maybe you'd like to gain 1,000 followers on your Facebook page or even have 1,000 new subscribers to your mailing list. That's great! Maybe there's a particular region in the world that you'd like to really target, or maybe you want to get reviews in as many places as possible. Fantastic! That's all measurable and tangible. List them in as straight forward a way as possible, and resist thinking small while still being realistic.

Next, take note of what your available assets are in order to attain these goals. If you're doing a plan for an album, then both the digital and physical copies of the album are assets. You'll likely want to have some sort of merch to sell such as t-shirts, which are also assets, and will help you in achieving your goal.

This is also a good time to analyse what other artists are doing that maybe you are not. Does their website or social media pages have something on them that you could also adapt and make your own? Maybe there is a certain structure or format that they are using that you find interesting. Are they collecting email addresses for email marketing or are they collecting Facebook Messenger signups? Or both? Do they run any kind of competitions, or do they give anything away? Really take a look at similar artists and borrow from them. You might even gain some inspiration for a totally unique idea that maybe you wouldn't have thought of otherwise!

Now for a timeline. It's important to set goals but you need to plan them all out in a logical and attainable way otherwise you're setting yourself up for failure. It's a standard practice in the music marketing industry to give yourself a three-month window in which to carry out the things in your marketing plan, so get them organised in ways that makes sense. For instance, in month one, it would make sense to have a giveaway in order to encourage people to sign up to your mailing list so that later you can tell them about your upcoming releases, tours, and more. If you wait until you release your album to get people to sign up for your mailing list then you've missed out on many opportunities to monetise your fan relationship.

Let me give you an example of a timeline I used for one of my projects. It encompassed a three-month time span after the release of a project:

Month one of Marketing plan for album starts

- Promotional video announcement goes out
- Give away live EP for free to people who sign up for or re-affirm their wishes to be on my mailing list through my website
- First Single is announced
- Launch new website
- Launch Facebook Page

Month two of marketing plan for album starts

- Launch new merch line
- Announce competition / giveaways
- Launch 30 second previews of all tracks

Month Three of Marketing plan for album starts

- Pre-buys on website start
- Pre-Save on Spotify / Apple Music start
- Launch new Album Packages (coupled with things like handwritten lyrics, signed photographs, physical copies of project, etc)
- Announce gig dates
- Album Released and DELUX version of album released (with 30 second "about these songs) included before each track on the album. Could also include live EP as bonus tracks here. Might also include demos and other unreleased material)

One month after release

- Announce winners of competition / giveaways
- Major press comes out / appearances
- Gigs galore

Two months after album release

- Release religious EP

Three months after album release

- Release "live EP" as a stand alone streaming only option

Everyone's A Damn Critic

As this book comes to a close, there is some more personal advice I'd like to give to you, artist to artist. Because you are a creative person, you are going to experience a lot of vulnerability. If you're not willing to be vulnerable, then you simply will not succeed as a creator. Author and public speaker Brené Brown puts it perfectly when she says, "if you're brave with your life and if you choose to live in the arena instead of the in the bleachers, then you're going to get your ass kicked. You're going to fall, you're going to fail, and you're going to know heartbreak. It's a choice...

today, choose courage over comfort". This is so perfect for you to remember. What you're doing is hard. There is no right or wrong way to achieve your definition of success there is only doing it. You can get advice from many people but only you can formulate your own opinions and make your own decisions. Get in the arena. It's scary. It's lonely. It's vulnerable. It's exciting!

People are going to listen to your music and say things like "I would've mixed that differently" or "that guitar part isn't right for the song". But you know what? It's your work - not theirs. It's easy to criticise and pick apart something that's already finished but let me tell you something - it's not so easy when you're creating something from nothing. Don't let it get to you. When this happens ask yourself if you were happy with the performance before this person criticised it. If so, then graciously take it on board but move on. I'm not saying that you should put blinders on and not take advice from trusted and verifiably experienced people but I would be willing to bet that this category of people was probably sought out for opinions during production and not after. If you didn't then maybe you need to ask yourself why you didn't. If you released something knowing that you didn't feel quite right about a certain aspect of it - and you didn't say anything at the time and you didn't ask the advice of a qualified and experience mentor - then you now own that screw up, my friend. And you have no one else to blame for it being in the final product. But thats okay - just don't do it again. Learn from it! Being in the drivers seat means celebrating your successes but it also means owning your failures, too.

What matters is that you protect your vulnerability by doing the best possible job you can do at this very moment in your life and that you relentlessly persevere until your project is finished. Then you can look back and recognise things that maybe you'd do differently in the future and recognise areas that you want to improve on. Until then, with every decision you make, I would encourage you to not put yourself in a position of regretting that you took an easier or cheaper option. If you can take a cheaper or easier option without sacrificing quality, then wonderful! If you have to delay releasing a project because it's going to cost you a bit more money and a bit more time to save up that money in order to make something better then absolutely do it! If you feel like re-recording a guitar part because you think the current part doesn't feel right - consult with your team about it. Don't ever put yourself in a position where you look back and wonder if something could've been better had you paid it a bit more TLC. Instead, put yourself in a position to say that you did absolutely everything you could at that moment in your life to create what you created and that's why it's perfect - flaws and all. Will you make mistakes - sure! Especially at the beginning. But that's okay. If you're making mistakes then you're pushing yourself out of your comfort zone and growing. If you can do that, than all the negative opinions of people who weren't in the arena with you absolutely do not matter and you can battle them by telling yourself that you did everything you could with the tools and knowledge and team that you had at the time. Good job, you!

Don't Forget WHY

As you attain your success and meet your milestones, sometimes your WHY can become a bit blurry. As we talked about before, your WHY will likely evolve as you do, but the underlying reason for WHY you got into the music business in the first place will not change. Your mission in the world will remain constant. Martin Luther King, Jr. was arguably the biggest leader in the United States civil rights movement, but no matter how famous he became, he never lost sight of the fact that injustice was still a problem, and that was why he was out there talking to the masses. The Walt Disney Company continues to grow into one of the world's biggest companies with hands in many different industries but they don't lose sight of the fact that in all that they do, they want to create the best family experiences possible. When a decision has to be made, they always fall back on that WHY for guidance. The most successful people or companies are steadfast in their WHY and never lose sight of it.

For me, as an artistic person, I want to do my part in making the world a more beautiful and happy place; to bring hope and inspiration to anyone looking for it. In everything that I do, from recording music to creating and running Dreamscope to writing this book, I constantly ask myself whether a particular activity I am doing is in support of my WHY. If it is, then I pursue that activity relentlessly, despite anyone telling me it's not possible for one reason or another.

Rejuvenate, Revitalise, Get Inspiration, and Repeat

As a creative person, you give a lot to the world and it can be exhausting in many ways. In order to continue being inspired and to create you must find time out for yourself regularly or you absolutely will get burnt out and burnout is not a fun thing to go through. Going to the gym every day is not only great for your physical body but it does wonders for your mind, too. Yoga and meditation are great at helping you to clear your mind. The world is full of noise and your mind is constantly receiving information. If you don't clear that information from your mind, then you will have no space for inspiration to take root and grow. Personally, I love going for long walks in one of the beautiful parks here in London where mobile phone reception is terrible and it's an absolute blessing. There are no advertisements, no shops, and because there is no mobile reception there is little contact with the outside world. I can simply get lost for a couple hours and maybe I choose to listen to music but maybe I just choose to listen to the sounds of the park instead. Whatever you choose to do, do it regularly and don't ever apologise for taking time for yourself. Ever.

When I was in my early 20's I was in Minnesota preparing for a central American tour that was going to be pretty tough in a lot of ways. I had just finished a year in high school, come off of another tour, released my very first album that was gaining national traction, finished taping a TV show for History Channel, appeared in an independent horror film, and did a radio commercial for United Way all within the span of two months and just before traveling to Minnesota for a gruelling two weeks of rehearsal. It was a lot and I felt the pressure to make it amazing because I had a lot of people who not only helped to make all of these things happen but there were a lot of people really depending on me, too. I was up late nearly every single night rehearsing, studying, running lines, practicing my blocking, and doing everything I could to not disappoint. Energy drinks were running through my veins by the time I was halfway through rehearsals for tour and, after a while, my body just gave out on me and I had to be flown back home where I was treated for exhaustion and diagnosed with chronic Epstein Barr syndrome. While it was humbling to be reminded of my own mortality, it was also a very helpless feeling to lose control of your mind and body. Trust me: don't do it. Take care of yourself.

After a project comes to an end, it is a great time to clear your mind for a few weeks. In fact you often need it. Allow yourself that time to breathe and to mentally have some closure with whatever it was you were doing so that you can clear the way for something new to begin. Once you've had your time of rejuvenation you will start to feel revitalised and inspiration can take root again. Next you know it, you'll be able to stimulate any inspiration that comes your way and suddenly you are ready to repeat this entire process again. It's important that you constantly review your WHY so that for every project you undertake you have clear direction for yourself and your team.

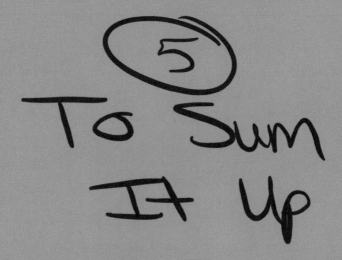

To Sum It Up

The truth is, 'making it' in the music industry isn't the same as it once was. The music industry in 2019 is not what it was in 1999 and it certainly won't be the same in 2039. The problem for the music industry is that consumers are demanding more of an experience with their music on their own terms and in ways that are unique to the individual. Try asking your friend to show you his or her music library and they will likely be slightly shy about it! This wasn't the case 50 years ago when music was much more of a social experience. To complicate matters even further, today's emerging artists' needs are constantly changing as well thanks not only to advances in technology but also in changes in our society and culture. In order for the music industry to be profitable again it has got to do better at adapting faster to these changes. It is worrisome to me that when I go to music industry events and talk to the very people who run the music industry's performing rights organisations, record labels, and media research companies only to hear them joke about how 'funny' it is that the industry is behind the curve. Then, in a presentation immediately following this jovial conversation, you hear the same big-wig executives whining about how things like piracy and lack of funding for the arts in education is ruining the music industry.

What these people do not understand is that anymore today, you as an artist and musician don't need them in the same way that you maybe did in 1999. You are able to learn how to record your own material and release it to the world simply by using an iPad just as bands like Gorillaz have done. You are able to reach, cultivate, and monetise relationships with fans from all corners of the globe. This doesn't mean that record labels are obsolete. Actually it's far from the truth and anyone who tells you that record labels are 'dead' or that you can 'be your own record label' is just flat out lying to you. It just means that record labels play a different role in the music landscape than they once did.

I believe you, the artist and the musician, are smarter than them. I believe you can see through the smoke and mirrors of companies promising you the flashy gimmicks that you can obtain on your own anyway. I believe you can see through the flashy recording studios and the incessant name dropping used as a tactic to prove their worth to you. I believe that if the music industry wants to secure its future then they need to invest in live music venues as a place for upcoming artists to find their footing. I believe the music industry needs to take a much larger role in the development of our future music business executives and future artists rather than leaving it to the already-overextended and cash-strapped education system. I believe that a record label's role has changed from one of selling to the consumer, thanks to consumers increasingly preferring to use third-party streaming apps, into one that operates as a service to the artist instead. As such, I believe that the artist is in a greater position now more than ever to demand more control over their work, under the guidance of a capable team, and in having that control, they must be willing to invest in their own careers and take a leading role in the selling of their music. We are in a different time and the music industry has got to get with it.

You play a big part in that change. You are smarter, more capable, and have access to more resources than any who have come before you. Stop limiting yourself and focusing on the things that get in the way of achieving your goals and focus instead on "how can I make this happen". Own your successes but don't be afraid of owning and learning from your failures, too, because failing only means that you were in the arena pushing your limits. In a music industry that you have helped to shape, you cannot get ahead if you aren't in the arena trying new things and doing things that once seemed

99

impossible. You have got to create your own opportunities for success and only you can define what that 'success' looks like.

Just remember that it all starts with WHY and that as you progress in your career, you only truly get so far from your past. In many ways, I'm still that young kid in Arizona, fighting tooth and nail to get any opportunity that comes my way. I'm ambitious, scared, excited, and uncertain all at the same time. I was fortunate to have great mentors, and I want to end our time here with an open letter to you, the new artists out there. I've been where you are. It's the kind of letter I wished I had had in my early years as a performer, and my great hope is that it will help you on your artistic journey.

Letter to a New Artist

Dear New Artist:

It's hard to know just where to begin, so I'll begin with this: please, for the sake of not only the continuation of culture and the beauty that music brings to a sometimes rotten world, but also for the sake of your own soul, do not give up. Perseverance isn't just a buzz word you hear in primary school. You're going to need it. It's going to take Tenacity. Grit. Endurance. Maybe even a certain blindness to the reality that the world wants to inflict on you. But you can do it. And, as the Dr. Seuss book says "oh the places you'll go"!

There really is no preparing you for the things that you'll encounter. But knowing your values, your morals, and being true to yourself will help. You'll need to learn how to hold yourself with dignity and pride even though, on the inside, you might be screaming and crying as you're being told that you're not good enough for one reason or another. Don't miss out on chance to escape to a room, alone, and let it out. Emotion is catharsis. Being an artist can be oppressive in many ways. But it's up to you to search for the beauty in it, too.

Don't ever forget that you have the chance to change lives through your music. And you will change lives, so long as you let your guard down enough to be vulnerable. Only then can the real emotions come out of you. More importantly, only then can others come to the realisation that they are not alone in how they feel as well. You are an artist, and as artists we are tasked with the burden of finding ways to express ourselves that others cannot, all with the hope that others are able to find peace even though it perhaps took you going through utter hell. It's easy to let the job become selfish. For many of us, writing and/or performing is therapy. That's okay, too.

You're going to get screwed over at one point or another. People are going to lie to you to get ahead. They are going to use you. Steal from you. Pick you apart just when you thought there was nothing left to shred. There really isn't anyway for you to totally prevent this, but you can lessen the blow by having a good group of people around you whether on your artist team or support from family and friends. The trick is learning to be vulnerable but never letting your guard down. It's a balance that might take you your whole career or life to find. That's okay, too. I believe you'll get there.

Force yourself to develop a hunger to learn and try new things. And never let yourself be afraid to fail, because failure is only another tool to help you to learn. If you fail at something, don't mope about it but do give yourself the time to try to understand the different reasons why something failed and either try again or move on to something new. But by allowing the fear of failure to prevent you from trying new things, you will never grow, you will never adapt, and you will become complacent. A wise woman once told me that being an artist is 99 percent business and only 1 percent singing, so make sure to fall in love with as much of that 99 percent as you possibly can.

You're really in for a wild ride, my friend! Full of ups and downs and twists that you won't be able to predict. You're going to find yourself in situations that make you stop and wonder "how the hell did I get here". You're going to work with people who are better than you. You're going to find yourself in rooms with high profile dignitaries, celebrities, and influencers, and you're going to tell yourself that you don't belong. The truth is that you do belong. You belong. Again: you belong. Just like those high profile people are making an impact on our culture and society, so too will your art. You are not an imposter and never will be. Keep telling yourself you're in those rooms for a reason and don't let the people standing there with you see your insecurities or intimidate you. Remain humble, but hold yourself high and wear a smile. Bask in the moment at every chance. You've earned it.

They say to those whom much is given, much is expected in return. Do the world a favour and take as many moments as possible to give back. Whether it's a lovely message to your team thanking them for their hard work, or using a project you're working on to raise awareness of an important cause. Art has always been used this way. It's important not to get so caught up in your career that you forget that there are others who weren't as lucky as you for one reason or another, and you now have a platform from which to give their voices flight. Others are going to live vicariously through you because maybe their circumstances prevented them from achieving the same things you have. Young children are going to look up to you and watch every move you make, every message you post on social media, and hang on every word you say. Make it all count. Not only because any amount of success can be taken away from you in an instant, but because you should aim to leave this world in a better place than you found it. You aren't working on an album. You are working on a legacy that will outlive you. You're a new artist now. But what do you want to be remembered for ultimately?

There is so much more I could tell you and warn you about. But that would take the surprise away. The fundamentals I've outlined in this letter, though, have helped me to get through some of the darkest times of my career, and they have also helped me in some of the most memorable moments, too. Keep your perspective, and hold it close. You have the potential to change someone's world through your music and that is a very magical experience.

I wish you good luck, my friend. Let your music soar and your passions reach the highest summit. The world needs you.

Musically Yours,
Matt

Just Thought You Should Know

Additional Resources

Further Reading

The following is a list of books that have had a profound impact on my career, and I know they will for you to! These are all on my personal recommended reading list – just thought you should know.

MUSIC BUSINESS

How Music Works	....	David Byrne
Music The Business: The Essential Guide To The Law And The Deals	....	Ann Harrison
This Business of Music: Definitive Guide to the Music Industry	....	M. William Krasilovsk Sidney Shemel John M Gross Jonathan Feinstein

SONGWRITING

101 Songwriting Wrongs and How To Right Them	....	Pat Luboff

MUSIC TECHNOLOGY

Modern Recording Techniques	....	David Miles Huber Robert E. Runstein

LIVE PERFORMANCE

How To Make Your Band Sound Great	....	Bobby Owsinski

MUSIC PUBLISHING

Music Money and Success: The Insiders Guide To Making Money In The Music Business	....	Jeff Brabec Todd Brabec

GENERAL BUSINESS AND MARKETING

Brand Famous: How To get Everyone Talking About Your Business .... Linzi Boyd

Feel The Fear And Do It Anyway .... Susan Jeffers

Ignore Everybody and 39 Other Keys To Creativity .... Hugh MacLeod

Start With Why .... Simon Sinek

The Tipping Point .... Malcolm Gladwell

Blank Contracts

Throughout the book I mention several different contracts that you should have in your arsenal for your artist business. You can download copies of these contracts in Word format at

www.dreamscopemediagroup.co.uk/contracts

Just Thought You Should Know

Appendix 1:
Sample Record Contract clauses

———————

While the sample given below is not a recording contract, the sections listed will very likely be included in any recording contract that you might receive. Of course, the contents of each section will change slightly depending on factors such as whether the contract is for a solo artist or for a band, the kind of recording contract that is being offered, the stage that the artist or band is in of their career, etc. It's also worth noting that most record companies are very protective over their contracts so it's nearly impossible to see an actual sample without breaking some kind of copyright law or non disclosure agreement. As always, you are strongly advised to seek the advice of a qualified attorney with experience working with music industry contracts before signing any agreement.

Introduction

This agreement (the "Agreement") is entered into between

_____

_____ ("Company") and

_____, known collectively as

_____ and performing

under the

name_____

(referred to as "Artist"). All references to "Artist" include all members of the group collectively and individually unless otherwise specified.

The parties agree as follows:

Exclusive Recording Services

During the Term (as described below), Artist will render recording services only for the Company and will not, under any other names or aliases and unless otherwise permitted under this Agreement, render recording services for any other party.

Master Recordings

Artist will deliver to Company technically and commercially satisfactory recordings containing not less than forty (40) minutes of playing time (the "Master Recording"). Company will release commercial products including physical products [Compact Discs], digital products [Downloads], or any other unforeseen means of distribution either technologically or physically which will embody the material contained on the Master Recordings (collectively, the "Records").

Term

The Artist's obligation to perform exclusive recording services begins on the latest signature date of this Agreement (the "Effective Date") and continues for 6 months after delivery of the first Master Recording (the "Term"). Artist grants to Company four options as part of this Agreement and the Company may extend the Term by exercising its option. If an option is exercised, the term will continue for 18 months after the delivery of the previous Master Recording ("Option Term"). If Company ever chooses not to exercise an option, the agreement will terminate regardless of how many options remain.

Grant of Rights

Artist assigns to Company all rights to the Master Recording in perpetuity. Artist grants to Company all right, title, and interest in the sound recording copyright (as provided under the U.S. Copyright Act of 1976 and international copyright treaties) to the Master Recordings, including:

the exclusive right to manufacture copies of all or any portion of the Master Recordings

Just Thought You Should Know

the exclusive right to import, export, sell, transfer, release, license, publicly perform, rent, and otherwise exploit or dispose of the Master Recordings, and

the exclusive right to edit, adapt, or conform the Master Recordings to technological or commercial requirements in various formats now known or later developed.

Territory

Artist grants Company World-wide rights (the "Territory").

Right to Use Artist's Name and Likeness

Company has the right to reproduce or distribute, in any medium, Artist's names, portraits, pictures, and likeness for purposes of advertising, promotion, or trade in connection with Artist or the exploitation of the Master Recordings and for any other purposes so to promote the interest and prestige of Company. Artist will be available from time to time to appear for photography, video performance, or the like, under the reasonable direction of Company. Artist is not entitled to any compensation for such services except for reimbursement of travel expenses.

Side-Artist Recording

Artist may perform as part of another artist's recording project (a "side−artist" performance) provided that Company has furnished written consent for such performance. Consent must not be unreasonably withheld. In the event of such performance, the following credit is included on the side−artist recording: "[Name of Artist] appears courtesy of [Company Name]."

Professional Name

With the exception of the Leaving Member sections of this Agreement, Artist will perform and record under the professional name _____ . Artist will not use a different name in connection with the Master Recordings unless Artist and Company mutually agree in writing.

Trademark Search

Company, at its discretion, may institute a search to determine whether there are any third-party uses for Artist's name. If the search indicates that the name cannot be used, Company and Artist will mutually agree on a substitute name. Any amounts up to but not exceeding _____ may be expended for the purposes of the trademark search and will be considered as a recoupable advance.

Production of Master Recordings

Artist is responsible for payment of all expenses incurred in the production of the Master Recordings and will obtain the appropriate permission, clearance, or release from any person or union who renders services in the production of the Master Recordings.

Subsequent Recording of Compositions

Artist represents and warrants that Artist will not record any composition contained on a Master Recording for a period of 5 years from the date of first release of a Company recording containing such composition.

Advances and Recoupable Costs

All money paid by Company to Artist, other than royalties paid under this Agreement, will be considered an advance against royalties ("Advances"). All Advances will be set off against future royalties. In connection with the initial Master Recording delivered, Company will pay Artist an Advance of _____ on the date of _____.

Advance for Option Term

In connection with the Master Recording delivered under the Option Terms, Company will pay Artist an Advance of _____.

Royalties

Company will pay Artist a percentage (the "Royalty") of the Company's sales for all Records as set forth:

Compact Discs. For Compact Discs sold, less the actual container costs (not to exceed 25% of SRLP), plus excise, sales, and similar taxes, Company will pay Artist __% of wholesale price.

Downloads. For Downloads, Company will pay Artist ___% of net receipts paid to Company regardless of the electronic mechanism for delivery.

Foreign Licenses

Company will pay Artist 50% of the net receipts paid to Company under any foreign license.

Compilations

If a composition from the Master Recording is used on a compilation or recording in which other artists are included, the Artist's royalty will be prorated. For example, if a composition from the Master Recording is included on a compilation containing nine selections from other artists, Artist shall be entitled to one-tenth (1/10th) of the royalty rate.

Flat Fee

Company will pay Artist ___% of the net receipts paid to Company under any flat fee license of the Master Recordings or any portion of the Master Recordings.

Promotional Recordings and Cutouts

No royalties will be due on Records furnished on a promotional basis. Nor will any royalty be due for Records sold by Company as cutouts or for scrap or otherwise on deletion from Company's catalog.

Statements; Audit

Company will pay Artist the Artist's Royalties within 30 days after the end of each quarter. Company will also furnish an accurate statement of sales of

Records during that month. Company will pay interest on any late payment from the due date until paid. The acceptance by Artist of any statement or payment does not prevent Artist's later questioning its accuracy. Company will keep accurate books of account covering all transactions relating to this Agreement. Artist or its representatives have the right on reasonable written notice to audit Company's books relating to the Records. If the audit indicates an underpayment greater than ____ for any six-month period, Company will pay for the audit.

Video

If Company decides during the term of this Agreement to produce one or more recordings combining the audio performance of Artist with a visual image (the "Video"), Company and Artist will mutually agree on the budget and production costs (the "Production Budget") for such Video or Videos. All sums paid by Company as part of the Production Budget will be considered as an Advance against royalties. Company is the sole owner of all worldwide rights to each Video, including the worldwide copyrights. Company has the right to use and allow others to use each Video for advertising and promotional purposes with no payment to Artist. "Advertising and promotional purposes" means all uses for which Company receives no money in excess of incidental fees such as tape stock and duplication and shipping. Artist is entitled to a royalty as established in the Royalty Section for all revenue derived from commercial exploitation of the Videos. Artist will issue a worldwide synchronisation license for any Controlled Compositions embodied on a Video. For a period of _____ years from the date of first release of any Video, Company has the right to allow others to use that Video for commercial purposes. If Company licenses or commercially exploits the Video(s), Company will pay, after deducting all costs advanced for production, a royalty of 50% of the net revenues from any license or sale of that Video. Artist grants to Company the right to synchronise the Master Recordings with visual images to create Videos.

111

Commercial Release of Records

Company will release the Records within 6 months of delivery of the Master Recordings (the "Guaranteed Release Date"). Artist will provide written notice if Company fails to release the recording by the Guaranteed Release Date. If, after 30 days from notification, Company has not released the recording, Artist may terminate this agreement and Artist may acquire the unreleased Master Recording and all related rights by paying to Company the sum of any advance for such Master Recording.

Artist Promotional Records

Company will furnish to Artist a total of 1000 promotional Records at no charge. Artist may obtain further Records from Company at Company's then-wholesale cost.

Album Artwork

Artist, at its own expense, may furnish camera-ready artwork for the Records at the time of delivery of the Master Recording. Such artwork may be delivered in electronic format. Company has the right to modify or conform the artwork to meet Company specifications and standards. However, Company will consult with Artist before making any modification. If Artist elects not to furnish artwork, Company will prepare the artwork and consult with Artist regarding the design. Company will advance the sum of _____ for artwork preparation. This payment is an advance against future royalties.

Artist Warranties

Artist warrants to Company that Artist has the power and authority to enter into this Agreement, is the Artist and copyright holder of the Master Recordings, or has or will obtain all necessary and appropriate rights and licenses to grant the license in this Agreement with respect to the Master Recordings. Artist warrants that the Master Recordings are original to Artist except for material in the public domain and such excerpts from other works that may be included with the written permission of the copyright owners, and that proper clearances or permission have been obtained from the artists of any copyrighted material, including but not limited to any digitally reprocessed samples of material incorporated in the Master Recordings. Artist warrants that Artist's use of any name or moniker will not infringe on the rights of others and that Artist's use of any musical composition or arrangement will not infringe on the rights of others.

Artist further warrants that the Master Recordings do not:
- contain any libellous material
- infringe any trade name, trademark, trade secret, or copyright, or
- invade or violate any right of privacy, personal or proprietary right, or other common law or statutory right.

Artist hereby indemnifies Company and undertakes to defend Company against and hold Company harmless (including, without limitation, attorney fees and costs) from any claims and damage arising out of a breach of Artist's Warranties as provided above. Artist agrees to reimburse Company for any payment made by Company with respect to this Section, provided that the claim has been settled or has resulted in a final judgment against Company or its licensees. Artist will notify Company in writing of any infringements or imitations by others of the Master Recording that may come to Artist's attention.

Controlled Compositions License

Artist grants to Company an irrevocable Universe wide license to reproduce all compositions wholly or partly written, owned, or controlled by Artist (the "Controlled Compositions"). Artist grants to Company a first mechanical license for all Controlled Compositions.

Mechanical Royalties

Artist acknowledges and agrees that Company will pay a royalty for the mechanical license on all Records manufactured for sale or commercial distribution at 75% of the minimum compulsory license rate (the

"Company Mechanical Rate") applicable in the country of manufacture. The applicable minimum statutory rate will be determined as of the date of the commencement of the recording of the applicable Master Recording. Mechanical Royalties are not payable for musical compositions of one minute or less in duration.

Leaving Members

If any member of Artist ceases to perform as a member of the group ("Leaving Member"), Artist will promptly give Company written notice. If the group disbands, each member of the group is considered to be a Leaving Member. Artist grants to Company an irrevocable option to engage the exclusive services of any Leaving Member as a recording artist. In the event of Company's exercise of this option, the Leaving Member will be considered to have entered into an agreement with Company on all the terms and conditions of this Agreement, including the initial term, the first option term, payments, royalties, and all other applicable terms. The Leaving Member will not, however, be responsible for any outstanding Artist debts, including unrecouped advances.

Termination

Company may terminate this Agreement within thirty (30) days of the expiration of the Term or any Option Period. Artist can terminate this Agreement if Company fails to pay Artist's Royalties when due or to accurately report Net Sales, if the failure is not corrected within 30 days after notice from Artist. If this Agreement is breached because of a failure to pay or accurately report royalties, all rights granted under this agreement revert to Artist, and Company will have no further rights regarding Artist or the Master Recordings.

If this Agreement is terminated for a reason other than Company's failure to pay or accurately report Artist's Royalties, the termination will not terminate the underlying license and copyrights granted to Company by Artist, nor Company's obligations to pay Royalties under this Agreement.

Termination in the Event of Leaving Member

Within ninety (90) days of receipt of notice of any Leaving Member, as defined in the Leaving Members section, Company will have the right to terminate the Agreement as to the remaining members of Artist. If that happens, all members of Artist will be deemed to be Leaving Members.

Mediation; Arbitration

If a dispute arises under this Agreement, the parties agree to first try to resolve the dispute with the help of a mutually agreed-on mediator in _____. Any costs and fees other than attorney fees will be shared equally by the parties. If it is impossible to arrive at a mutually satisfactory solution within a reasonable time, the parties agree to submit the dispute to binding arbitration in the same city or region, conducted on a confidential basis under the laws of _____. Any decision or award as a result of arbitration will include the assessment of costs, expenses, and reasonable attorney's fees and a written determination of the arbitrators. Absent an agreement to the contrary, arbitration will be conducted by an arbitrator experienced in music industry law. An award of arbitration is final and binding on the Artist and may be confirmed in a court of competent jurisdiction. The prevailing party has the right to collect from the other party its reasonable costs and attorney fees incurred in enforcing this agreement.

General

Nothing contained in this Agreement makes either Company or Artist a partner, joint venturer, or employee of the other party for any purpose. This Agreement may not be amended except in a writing signed by both parties. No waiver by either party of any right is a waiver of any other right. If a court finds any provision of this Agreement invalid or unenforceable as applied to any circumstance, the remainder of this Agreement will be interpreted to carry out the intent of the parties. This Agreement is governed by and interpreted in accordance with the laws of

Just Thought You Should Know

_____. This Agreement expresses the complete understanding of the parties on the subject matter and supersedes all prior proposals, agreements, representations, and understandings. Notices required under this Agreement can be sent to the parties at the addresses provided below. In the event of any dispute arising from or related to this Agreement, the prevailing party is entitled to attorney's fees.

Appendix 2:
Commentary on Record Contract clauses

Below is a brief commentary about each recording contract clause that I included in Appendix 1. Please remember that I am not an attorney and that you should always seek the advise of a qualified lawyer with experience working on music industry contracts. This is simply from my experience dealing with recording contracts and music lawyers but I just thought you should know, too.

Introduction
This section simply specifies that the contract will be entered into by the entity acting as the record label and the artist or band and could see alterations depending on whether or not the record label was signing an artist or a larger ensemble like a band. It is important, in a situation where a band or large ensemble is being signed, to include the individual names of those who are part of the ensemble as well as the name they collectively go by. These details are important because it is not unusual for an artist or band to use an alias like in the case of Alecia Beth Moore who performs under the name P!nk. This is brought up again later in the contract in greater detail.

Exclusive Recording Services
It was important to specify that it would be a breach of contract if the artist were to record with another company even if it is under a different name. Examples of this would be Prince who went by several aliases, which

included a symbol that the media translated into the name The Artist Formerly Known As Prince, so that he was able to work outside of the requirements of his contract with Warner. This section ties into the section of the contract where it is agreed what name the artist or band will perform under.

Master Recordings

When entering into a recording contract, it is important to specify the expected length of the master recordings and what you intend to do with it after the artist has turned that in to the label. To secure the company's rights to reproduce the master recording today as well as in the future, it is important to indicate that there could be other means of carrying out the record label's prerogative utilising methods that are not known at the time that the contract was written.

The Term

Essential to any contract, it must specify the amount of time that the contract can be enforced. This section also specifies the number (if any) of options the record label is entitled to which would extend the contract a specified amount of time. Options are essential to a record company mainly because it isn't uncommon for a new artist, especially, to achieve recoupment and therefore the record label may enforce its option in an effort to make more of its money back.

Grant of Rights

Along with a section that explains what the record label intends to do with the master recording, it is also important to specify that the artist must give the record label certain rights in order for it to carry out its intentions. In addition to this, it is important to specify the length of time the artist is granting these rights to the record label. Standard practice is for record labels to be granted these rights "in perpetuity" or forever although this may be negotiable if you have some clout in the industry.

Territory

After granting these rights to the company, it's important to specify where these rights will be enforced. Some contracts are now starting to grant universe-wide rights with the anticipation that one day, humans will be based in many different parts of the universe.

Right to Use Artist's Name and Likeness

This section is what allows the record company to essentially license the artist's name and likeness in connection with the promotion and overall image of the album. Its important that the section set the expectation that the artist would need to be available to take photographs for the album cover and artwork as well as for any promotional photographs that may be used online and in promotion of the album. In addition to the promotion and creation of the album, the record label should also have the ability to use the artist's likeness in connection with the promotion of the record label. In the book Music Business Agreements by Richard Bagehot and Nicholas Kanaar, the authors state that the record label should have "complete freedom to utilise names and likeness for all it's purposes and not just directly in connection with the sale of the artist's records" in an effort to increase it's own profile.

Side-Artist Recording

Side-artist recording has to do with an artist who is under an exclusive contract however wishes to appear on other recordings released by another record label. This could be as a duet with another artist, as a background singer, or as a session musician. In some instances it may be beneficial for the record label to allows this and usually is the signed artist simply has to get written permission in order to do so.

Trademark Search

This section is not always necessary. If it were a band that I was signing it may be a more relevant section because bands use names that they've made up and there is a risk that another band or organisation might be using it

Just Thought You Should Know

already. However, if it were a solo artist using his or her own name it might be unnecessary to include this provision because it is not likely that someone else is using the name. This, of course, could change if the name were more common.

Production of Master Recordings

In this example I have specified that the artist or band is responsible for the expenses in producing the Master Recording because they are being granted an advance directly. Sometimes the record label will pay the studio, producer, musicians and all other costs directly to the source but as an independent record label it is more feasible to pay the band or artist and leave it to them to pay the parties involved in the making of the Master Recordings.

Subsequent Recording of Compositions

Without exclusivity, other parties could issue competing versions of an artist's recordings, with resultant confusion. Therefore, this section is important and allows the record label to exclusively exploit a particular composition without the interference of another version of the song that could adversely affect the label's income stream.

Advances and Recoupable Costs and Advances for Option Term

In any recording contract, an artist is particularly interested in these two sections because it is where the record label explains the amount of any advances that are going to be given and when they will be given, if any.

Royalties, Foreign Licenses, Compilations, Flat Fee, Promotional Recordings

A company may use the Suggested Retail List Price (SRLP) system or a percentage of the wholesale price when paying royalties. However, most contracts use the Suggested Retail List Price (SRLP).

Statements; Audit

This section is vital and the important thing to watch out for is simply the number of days the record company has to pay their artist, which is typically either 30 or 90.

Commercial Release of Records

Having the record label guarantee a release time frame protects the artist. If a situation arises where the album is not released in the specified time then the artist may demand that the master recording rights be transferred to them. However, many labels will want to have any advances repaid before the rights are transferred.

Artist Warranties

As a record label this section is very important although it is not always present in contracts. It is essentially a list of promises that the artist is making to the record label and if the promises are broken then the artist indemnifies the record label and agrees to pay for the record label's damages caused as a result of the artist's infringement.

Controlled Compositions License and Mechanical Royalties

Controlled Compositions License is where the artist is telling the record label that he or she is granting them the first chance to reproduce their compositions. The Mechanical Royalties provision explains how the artist is compensated as a result of them granting these rights to the label.

Leaving Members

Under this provision, the label makes known it's right to obtain a recording contract with any member of the band or artist's musicians upon their departure from the group. A label may modify the provision so that they can recoup what the band owes from the leaving member making the leaving member stuck with the band's debts.

Termination

It is essential in any contract that both parties understand the circumstances in which they may terminate the contract. As an artist it is important that some kind of language be included requiring the record label to pay royalties within a certain time frame or their livelihood could be at stake. If there is a circumstance where the label does not pay royalties to an artist, and after being notified in writing that they were late, then it is common for the rights granted under the agreement to then revert to the artist.

Termination in the event of a Leaving Member

This provision relates to the previous one regarding leaving members except that this one gives the company the right to terminate the contract if a member of the band leaves.

Mediation; Arbitration

Another essential part of the recording contract, this allows the parties in the contract the opportunity to deal with disputes in an easier and more affordable manner. The independent record company would want to have the mediator located in the same city so they are able to avoid additional fees for travel. The location of the mediator and the locale whose laws bind the arbitration are intentionally left blank in this contract and would be filled in prior to delivery of the contract to the artist or band.

General

This is a boilerplate, or standard, provision, which establishes certain rules that can affect how resolutions are made and which court will enforce the provisions that are contained within the contract.

Glossary

80:20 Rule

A term attributed to an Italian economist Vilfredo Pareto. When applied to business the 80:20 rule says that 80% of your business will come from 20% of your customers.

360 Degree Record Deal

A type of exclusive recording contract between an artist or band and a record label that, in addition to income from music sales and on an exclusive basis, gives the record label a percentage of income from all of the artist or band's entertainment-related revenue streams even if those revenue streams are outside of the music industry.

Achievement Motivation

A drive some people have to pursue and attain challenging goals. They wish to achieve objectives and advance up the ladder of success.

Affiliation Motivation

A drive to relate to people on a social basis – to work with compatible people and experience a sense of community. These people work better when they are complimented for their favourable attitudes and cooperation. They tend to surround themselves with friends and likeable people.

Chorusing

An effect used especially when recording music that occurs when several sounds with the same or nearly the same pitch and time are combined.

Click-through Rate

This is a ratio that shows the number of users who clicked on a specific link compared to the total number of people who viewed a specific page, email, or advertisement.

Just Thought You Should Know

Clipping

Put simply, this is when audio distorts due to being amplified beyond it's maximum limit.

Compression

A type of dynamic processing that reduces the dynamic range of a certain track, sound, or of the overall song itself. It can also be used to increase the perceived level while still maintaining the overall sound of the track.

Condenser Microphone

A microphone typically used in a recording studio setting that has the ability to capture a larger frequency range, are more sensitive to loud sounds, and generally have a louder output. They require external power, such as phantom power, in order to operate. It consists of two charged plates: one movable diaphragm and one fixed.

Copyright

The legal right to sell, reproduce, or licence a piece of work. This can include work such as a piece of writing, a photograph taken, a drawing, or a recording. In many countries, particularly those who are signatories of the Berne Convention, copyright is automatic once a piece of work is created. However, in some cases, formal copyright registration may be recommended.

Copyright Assignment

When a copyright owner transfers to another person or organisation all of or a specified number of the copyright controls granted to him/her as the copyright owner of a piece of work. Also referred to as an assignment of copyright.

Copyright Controls

The specific control that a copyright owner has over the piece of work he/she created. These include:

- Reproduction rights
- Distribution rights
- Rental rights

- Adaptation rights
- Performance rights
- Communication rights

DAW

The abbreviation for "Digital Audio Workstation".

Delay

When used in digital audio mixing, audio is stored directly into the computer's RAM and then read out again at a pre-defined length of time. This, then, can be repeated to add complexity to the delay.

Demographics

Characteristics of a population such as age, income, sex, education level, marital status, religion, etc.

Digital Aggregator

A company who distributes audio files to digital stores and streaming outlets. These companies are different from a distributor in that they generally anyone can use their services. They make their money from upfront fees and/or charging a percentage of sales.

Digital Audio Workstation

Software and, sometimes, an electronic device, that is used for recording and editing audio.

Domain

Explained simply, a domain, commonly referred to as an "internet domain" or "domain name", it is the web address used to access a particular website. Example: www.dreamscopemediagroup.com

Dynamic Microphone

Arguably the microphone with the most diverse kind of uses, this kind of microphone is incredibly durable and operates using electromagnetic induction. Inside contains two magnets and a piece of moving coil placed in between them which generates the electrical current as sound hits it.

Dynamic Range

The changes in a sound or recording from it's loudest points to it's softest.

Just Thought You Should Know

Electromagnetic Induction

When a piece of electrically conductive metal cuts across the flux lines of a magnetic field, current is generated within the metal.

Electronic Press Kit

A collection of promotional materials combined in a single and easy to distribute electronic file for the purposes of showing anyone in the music industry who an artist is, what they have done and/or are doing, and their contact details.

Electrostatic Principle

Where two plates, one of them flexible, are placed within a space and charged. Sound passing in between these plates alters the space between them, changing the voltage and creating signal.

EPK

The abbreviation for "Electronic Press Kit".

Facebook Pixel

An analytics code created by Facebook that can be hidden on a website to track website visitors and their behaviours.

Google Tracking ID

An analytics code created by Google that can be hidden on a website to track website visitors and their behaviours.

IFPI

The abbreviation for "The International Federation of the Phonographic Industry".

Intellectual Property

Property that is owned by a person or organisation that results from some kind of creative work such as writing a book, writing / recording a song, creating a logo, taking a picture, making a film, etc. This includes any patents or copyrights.

International Federation of the Phonographic Industry

The non-profit organisation registered in Switzerland that represents the interests of the global recording industry.

International Standard Recording Code

An unique code assigned to a single recording that is used internationally for identifying that specific recording.

IP

The abbreviation for "Intellectual Property".

ISRC

The abbreviation for "International Standard Recording Code".

Limiting

A type of dynamic processor that is used in audio production to keep a sound's peak volume from passing a specified point.

Master Recording

The first recording of a mixed and mastered song from which all other copies are made.

Messenger Bot

An automated chat used within Facebook's Messenger platform designed to respond to a user through a guided conversation.

Microphone preamp

An external device used in conjunction with a microphone that amplifies the signal and adds characteristics to the sound.

Microphone

A type of transducer used in audio production to capture acoustic sound and convert it into electricity which then can be amplified for recording and/or editing.

Niche Marketing

Marketing and selling a product or service to a very specific and narrow segment of the population.

One Sheet

A single sheet that is helpful in the promotion of a particular project and that contains brief information about an artist, information about the release, and contact details.

Performing Rights Organisation

An organisation that protects the rights of copyright holders and acts as the intermediary in the collection of and distribution of royalties between someone wishing to use copyrighted material in public and the copyright owner.

Phantom Power

Supplied from an external device such as recording or mixing console, turning on phantom power sends +48 volts of DC power through an XLR cable to power another device such as a condenser microphone.

Power Motivation

The drive to influence people, take control and change situations. These people wish to make an impact on their organisation. People who seek institutional power have the need to influence other's behaviour for the good of the organisation however people who seek personal power tend to lose the trust and respect of a team making them unsuccessful leaders.

PRO

The abbreviation for "Performing Rights Organisation".

Project-Specific Recording Deal

A type of recording contract between an artist or band and a record label that is usually based on the completion of a single project.

Psychographics

Used in marketing to identify the personality, attitudes, and tastes of a specific segment of the population.

Publishing Administration

The administration, registration and licensing of compositions, as well as the collecting of publishing royalties, on behalf of a composer or another publisher.

Reverb

Short for reverberation, reverb, as it's commonly referred to, is caused when a sound is reflected continually, which it will continue to do until the sound is absorbed by the surfaces and/or objects in the room.

Ribbon Microphone

Works using electromagnetic induction like a dynamic microphone except that the moving coil is replaced by a very fine (and delicate) piece of ribbon to generate current.

Search Engine Optimisation

The process of ensuring that a particular website appears higher in search engine results with the objective of achieving higher visitors to that website.

SEO

The abbreviation for "Search Engine Optimisation".

Short URL

A substantially shorter web address that redirects to a previously specified and longer web address.

Signal Flow

The flow of audio beginning from the point that a sound is produced and continuing as it changes forms and is passed through different electronic devices, altered, and finally reproduced in a manner than can be heard by the human ear. Usually depicted in visual form by a kind of line graph.

Stage Plot

A graphic representation depicting the overhead view of a stage and the placement of the various instruments, musicians, speakers, etc. that are on it.

Term of Copyright

The length of time a person, persons, or organisation may legally hold the copyright of a piece of creative work. Countries who are signatories to The Berne Convention agree that the term of copyright lasts at least 50 years after the author's death however countries are free to make longer terms. For instance, in the United States and in the European Union, copyright lasts for the duration of the author's life plus 70 years.

The Berne Convention

An international treaty originally established in 1886 in Switzerland that is now agreed to by 177 countries world-wide. According to the treaty, if a copyright exists in one country, then it is also valid in all of the member countries who are signatories.

Time-based Effects

A category of effects that can be added to a sound to alter it such as reverberation, delay or chorusing.

Trademark

Symbols, words, or the combination of that are legally registered as representing a specific brand and/or product or service.

Transducer

Something such as a microphone, a guitar, a speaker, and even the human ear that changes one form of energy into another corresponding form of energy.

Universal Product Code

Commonly referred to as a "barcode", this widely used in countries around the world to track trade items. It consists of 12 numeric digits along with a corresponding machine-readable barcode.

UPC

The abbreviation for "Universal Product Code".

XLR

Sometimes referred to as a microphone cable or a balanced cable, it is commonly used in live and studio productions because it produces the clearest possible sound. It contains three wires and therefore has three pins at the end; two that carry the signal and one that acts as a neutral ground.

Printed in Poland
by Amazon Fulfillment
Poland Sp. z o.o., Wrocław